THE

THE TEACHING OF THE HEART

in three cycles of manifestation
of the Ray of Love-Wisdom:

I

Leaves of Maitreya's Garden
The Call of the Heart
The Illumination of the Heart
The Heart of the Community
The Heart of Infinity
The Fiery Hierarchy
The Fiery Heart
The World of Fire
The Prayer of the Heart
Brotherhood

II

Blossoms of Maitreya's Garden
The Sun of Love
The Joy of the Heart
The Rainbow of Fire

III

Fruits of Maitreya's Garden
The Fruit of Love

THE CALL OF THE HEART
Heralding the Coming of the Messiah

THE TEACHING OF THE HEART

BOOK 1

ZINOVIA DUSHKOVA

Radiant Books
Moscow

Copyright © 2016 by Zinovia Dushkova and Alexander Gerasimchuk

This book was originally published in Russian as part of Volume 1 of *Uchenie Serdtsa* by Zvezda Vostoka, Moscow, in 2004. Copyright © 1998, 2001, 2004 by Zinovia Dushkova. Translated from the Russian by Alexander Gerasimchuk with John Woodsworth, Member of the Literary Translators' Association of Canada. Translation of introduction edited by Shelley Fairweather-Vega and John Woodsworth.

All rights reserved. No part of this book may be used or reproduced in any manner whatsoever without written permission from the publisher except in the case of brief quotations embodied in critical articles and reviews. For additional information, please contact *info@radiantbooks.org*.

Note on language: To refer to a human being of any gender, this book uses the word *man*, which has its roots in the Sanskrit *manu* ("thinking creature"), and the pronouns *he*, *him*, and *his* accordingly. This is not intended to exclude women, but simply to ensure readability and clarity, since gender-neutral language can sometimes be cumbersome and confusing.

Publisher's Cataloging-In-Publication Data

Names: Dushkova, Zinovia. | Gerasimchuk, Alexander, translator. | Woodsworth, John, translation editor.
Title: The call of the heart : heralding the coming of the Messiah / by Zinovia Dushkova ; translated from the Russian by Alexander Gerasimchuk with John Woodsworth.
Other titles: Uchenie Serdtsa. English | The teaching of the heart
Description: First English edition. | Moscow : Radiant Books, 2016. | Series: The teaching of the heart ; book 1. | Includes bibliographical references. | "This book was originally published in Russian as part of Volume 1 of *Uchenie Serdtsa* by Zvezda Vostoka, Moscow, in 2004."
Identifiers: ISBN 978-5-9908268-1-6 (paperback) | ISBN 978-5-9908268-2-3 (e-book)
Subjects: LCSH: Spiritual life. | Messiah. | Heart. | Love—Philosophy. | BISAC: BODY, MIND & SPIRIT / Inspiration & Personal Growth. | BODY, MIND & SPIRIT / General. | SELF-HELP / Spiritual.
Classification: LCC BF624 .D8813 2016 | DDC 204/.4—dc23

British Library Cataloguing-in-Publication Data

A catalogue record for this book is available from the British Library.

First English Edition
published in 2016 by Radiant Books,
an imprint of Dushkova Publishing, LLC   ISBN 978-5-9908268-1-6 (pbk)
www.radiantbooks.org   ISBN 978-5-9908268-2-3 (ebk)

*The Resurrected Christ descends from Heaven
astride the White Steed as the Kalki Avatar
and appears in the Image of the Great Buddha,
uniting in Himself the Mahdi and Saoshyant,
as well as all the Saviours of the Human Race,
under the Name of Maitreya meaning "Love."
Let us accept the Call coming from the Heart
of the Lord of Love and Compassion —
the Messiah, who has come to us from above.*

CONTENTS

The Greatest Teacher and His Teaching................... ix
  Maitreya: The Messiah of All Times and Peoples ix
  Modern Spiritual Books: Preparation of Humanity for the New Age xv
  The Fiery Experience: The Divine Inspiration of All Sacred Scriptures xx
  The Great Mystery: The Triune Teaching of Maitreya xxiv
  The Mystery of Light: The Advent of the Messiah....................................... lii

Appeal to Humanity lxxi

The Call of the Heart 1
  Part I 3
  Part II 75

Notes 183
Glossary 199
About the Author..205

THE GREATEST TEACHER AND HIS TEACHING
by Alexander Gerasimchuk

MAITREYA
The Messiah of All Times and Peoples

EVERY POPULATED WORLD has a Lord. His Divine Spirit has passed through countless human existences in all possible forms and manifestations in different worlds over many and many billions of years. When man reaches the level of Divinity destined for every human spirit, the time comes for him, through a Great Sacrifice, to become a Creator of a new world in the boundless Universe, according to the reigning Cosmic Laws.

In our Galaxy of the Milky Way is to be found one of the most ancient highly spiritual civilizations, which is located in the constellation of Canis Major with Sirius as a central star. This civilization plays a large role in creating life in other star systems throughout the Milky Way, being dominant among seven constellations. After passing through their own evolution and reaching its apex, the Children of this Star stepped into the vast expanses of the Cosmos in order to found a new life.

Thus, at the dawn of the Grand Cycle of Evolution, one of them, whose true Name cannot be pronounced, has become the Creator, Preserver, and Transfigurer of the Solar System. People have given Him many Names: Maitreya, Christ, Buddha, Vishnu, Ra, Allah, and so on, or, simply, God.

Together with Him from the Distant Worlds also came the Seven Sons of Light, who became the Regents of planets. Billions of years ago, when our Earth was still only at the stage of formation, they had already descended on her "firmament" to prepare conditions for a new life and a new humanity. As soon as the conditions became suitable, sixty billion human seeds of spirit, begotten in the Seven Rays of the Solar Hierarch, filled all the earthly spheres. Thus, He became a Cosmic Father for all humankind on the Earth.

The continents of the planet were divided into seven spheres between the Seven Sons, the Great Teachers. Each of them represents one of the Seven Rays, bearing certain energies, in which the humanity of the entrusted territories develops. Yet there is one continent that has existed from the beginning and has never shared the fate of the others. On this Sacred Island, the Great Teachers founded the Brotherhood of Light, known as Shambhala. Being the cradle of the first man, Shambhala has made its mark in many legends of the world as something fabulously beautiful and accessible only to a very few: the White Island, the City of Gods, Mount Meru, the Pure Land, the Garden of Eden, and so on. The Solar Hierarch is the permanent Head of Shambhala, being a Master for the Seven Teachers — that is, the Teacher of Teachers. But for each period of time, in accordance with evolutionary tasks, He designates one of them as the Ruler of Shambhala.

According to the Cosmic Laws, every Creator must try and experience His own creation, for which He is responsible in the eyes of the Universe. And so, during each new stage of evolution, the Solar Hierarch gave a giant fiery impetus for the development of the planet, incarnating Himself amidst humankind on the Earth. In all the ancient religions of the world, He was revered as the Supreme God, personifying the Sun. Also many legends and myths have preserved the lore about the descent of Gods from the mysterious star Sirius. Even the Great Pyramid of Giza was built in such a way that once a year, on 19 July, the Day of the God Ra, Sirius appears in a vertical corridor and illuminates its inner sanctum, where ancient mysteries took place. In modern religions He has become a Mysterious Spirit, about whom little is known, but who rules over all that exists: Sanat Kumara, Chakravartin, and the Ancient of Days.

There is no people in the world among which He would not incarnate Himself as an ordinary human being. Each time His path was hard, because humanity could not stand His Light hidden under earthly clothes, and treated Him cruelly. But the goal of the Solar Hierarch has always been the same: to help people realize their divine nature.

However, at the beginning of the present evolutionary cycle of humanity, after His Power and Might established the current position of the Earth, He stepped aside to allow the planet to develop according to her own laws, until a new Cosmic Period comes, signifying a change of cycles. The Solar Hierarch entrusted the heavy burden of the world to His Eldest of the Seven, the Greatest Son of Light — to the Lord Morya, who is the bearer of all Seven Rays and who essentially is one and inseparable with His Father. And since Morya is the Eldest, He is also a Teacher for the other Teachers. From now on only partial manifestations of the Solar Hierarch would enlighten the earthly incarnations of His Sons, who composed Images of the one and same Divine Spirit, such as Rama, Krishna, Moses, Solomon, Zoroaster, Gautama Buddha, Lao-Tzu, Confucius,

Jesus Christ, Muhammad, and many other prophets and saints.

Nevertheless, humankind's faith that their beloved God of Sun would once again return to the Earth was so strong that, passing from generation to generation, it had become ingrained in all the beliefs of the peoples of the world, which later, through thousands and thousands of years, would form the basis of modern religions. So, every religion awaits Him — the Messiah and the Saviour — and names Him in its own way, forgetting that all these wonderful Names belong to the same Divine Spirit they await: Christ of Christianity, Maitreya of Buddhism, the Mahdi of Islam, the Kalki Avatar of Hinduism, the Messiah of Judaism, Saoshyant of Zoroastrianism, Li Hong of Taoism, the Divine Sage of Confucianism, and many folk beliefs about a Hero-Saviour who will return once again, such as, for example, King Gesar or King Arthur.

Two thousand years ago, the time came for the Earth to start fulfilling the task of Love-Wisdom, in whose Rays the Solar Hierarch brought forth the entire System. With the aim of sowing the first seeds of Divine Love by human hands and feet on earthly soils, His Son — Jesus — was born on the planet. He was not the Messiah promised in all religions, but in Him, as in no other, was manifested the Power and Might of His Father — Christ the Sun.

However, people committed the most terrible crime in relation to Jesus Christ, sentencing Him to death and crucifixion on a cross. According to Cosmic Laws, humankind and the planet which treated this man with such cruelty — the man in whom the God who had given them life was manifested — were no longer suitable for further evolution and were to suffer capital punishment, annihilation. Yet the Great Love of Christ, His Hope and Faith in humanity, saved the planet from the sentence the Earth-dwellers had brought down on themselves. Christ postponed it by His Will until the Cosmic Period comes when His Father, the Solar Hierarch Himself, will be able to incarnate Himself on the Earth. During this time humanity was to realize the gravity of its crime and to atone for it in the way as Jesus Christ taught: by Love.

It should be said this heinous crime has not passed without a trace for the future of earthlings. The problem is that humanity, after crucifying Jesus Christ in whom the Solar Hierarch was manifested, made it clear that they no longer need a God in human flesh, and deprived Him of the Right to be incarnated in a physical body. Of course, He could enlighten the purest and worthiest people by His Ray, who then could be fairly considered His partial incarnations on the Earth. However, His personal incarnation in a human body, as it used to be in antiquity, can no longer occur. Hence the appearance of statements of the most enlightened people that the Second Coming of Christ should be expected in the Spirit, rather than as an ordinary mortal man.

MODERN SPIRITUAL BOOKS
Preparation of Humanity for the New Age

THE ADVENT OF MAITREYA on the Earth means the start of the New Age, which supposes spiritual awakening. To prepare humanity for this amazing time, many beautiful souls have been incarnated to bring new ideas to the world in all spheres of life. That is why, especially now, at the junction of two Eras, many books of spiritual content have appeared, designed to shift the consciousness of humanity. However, since everyone is on their own level of development — what is clear to one may be quite unclear to another — the quality of these books represents all levels of consciousness, from the lowest to the highest. But their essential task is always the same — to encourage as many people as possible to take the path of Love, Good, and Light. Obviously, if such a goal is not evident throughout the course of a book, then it cannot be regarded as spiritual.

There are a great many techniques for writing such unusual books, and in each case they are individual. Nevertheless, it is possible to classify them all into four main groups that are known to esoteric philosophy: spiritual enlightenment, mediumship, mediatorship, and the Fiery Experience.

The first method of writing is characteristic of ordinary people without any extraordinary abilities. But they aspire to the Light, and their high level of spirituality awakens their *Chalice* of accumulations, the experience of many past lives that practically everyone possesses. After all, many people follow the path of Light not for only one lifetime; they could have, for example, passed an Initiation in an ancient civilization, studied some secret books of the past, they could have been close to Jesus Christ and Gautama Buddha, and so on. And in moments of illumination and enlightenment, memories from the Chalice might have developed into a new understanding of the sacred texts, as well as into beautiful mystical and spiritual novels, which awaken the imagination of readers and impel them towards the unusual. Of course, authors may even be unaware that their books describe one of the pages of their lives, perhaps even the start of their path towards the Light, which now serves as an inspiration for many other people.

A medium is an intermediary between the physical world and the near-Earth layers of the Subtle World. Mediums are born with this ability; but if they do not aspire towards the Light, then the information transmitted through them is in constant danger of being influenced by dark forces. On the other hand, mediators and fiery yogis have to *become* such.

Mediators are individuals who have accumulated significant experience serving the Light throughout their previous lives. Their elevated morality and merit of the past allow them to obtain access to the spatial Treasury of high spheres and draw knowledge from there, or to communicate with high spirits or even with highly developed extra-terrestrial civilizations who want to help humankind on the Earth. In modern language, a mediator can be called a *conscious channeller*. Any medium, provided they are morally pure and strive towards the Light, can become a mediator. Since mediators possess a high level of spiritual accumulations, they can also consciously communicate with their own spirits, their Divine Selves, receiving clear answers to various questions. This, of course, cannot be regarded as channelling. High mediators are able to reach many degrees of the next stage, that of the fiery yoga; only the highest degrees, such as the ability to fly to Distant Worlds and Cosmic Co-operation with the Forces of Light, will be unavailable to them. Yet even these restrictions are in force only until the mediators reach that level of spirituality which opens such opportunities.

However, it should be borne in mind that the information passing through mediators, i.e., through their own levels of earthly understanding, may be distorted. That is why the Great Teachers do not use this method to transmit Teachings. Only in a few cases, when the spiritual purity of the mediators is at a sufficiently high level, can they work in the Rays of one of the Teachers or with their authorized disciples. Edgar Cayce, being an exceptional man of high morals, is an example of such a mediator, who, moreover, was under the guidance of the Forces of Light.

The Great Teachers have quite a lot of advanced disciples, who are permitted to work with humanity through mediators and to act on behalf of the Teachers. As a rule, these disciples are in a disembodied state, staying close to their Masters in the higher spheres of the Subtle World. One might say that in this way, they are practising to attain the degree of Teacher. Studying with the Great Teachers is largely an expression of free will. The Teacher simply indicates a goal, but how disciples achieve it is their own decision. The same applies to the comprehension of Truth: disciples can gather its fragments, which are scattered through all the sacred texts, and only if they themselves come to a correct conclusion can the Teacher confirm it. Hence, how exactly disciples work with humanity and undertake their "practicum" depends upon their own free will;

and sometimes it may be that they, like all people who learn, make insignificant mistakes.

There is a custom in the East: when Teachers accept disciples, they must renounce their own names and take that of their Teachers. These names may represent either the current names of the Teachers or the names of their previous earthly incarnations. That is why there are so many various messages from the "Ascended Masters" now, the quality of which largely depends upon the purity of the receivers' consciousness. It should also be borne in mind that, in the near-Earth layers of the Subtle World, there are many disembodied souls, the so-called impersonators, who pretend to be the Teachers or their disciples, but have quite different goals. Therefore, one should discern such moments and judge any spiritual book simply by such criteria as: Has it brought one joy and spiritual awakening? Has it encouraged one to do good deeds in respect to other people? Has it impelled one to set out on the path of self-sacrificing service to the Light? If yes, then it has come from the Light, and one should not listen to those who do not share one's opinion; yet at the same time one should not condemn those books that have left one indifferent, but moved other people closer to the Light.

The Teachers themselves choose one or two people and work with them in a certain Ray of the Hierarchy with the purpose of advancing the consciousness of humanity to a new level every Eastern century, which consists of sixty years. During this time, mediators can connect to this single Stream, receiving some information and transmitting it through their own consciousness.

THE FIERY EXPERIENCE
The Divine Inspiration of All Sacred Scriptures

THE FIERY EXPERIENCE is the method which the Great Teachers use to transmit the Supreme Knowledge through their colleagues and disciples who practise the fiery yoga. Perhaps, when seeing the word *yoga*, the reader imagines a person sitting in the lotus position, but this has no relationship to the yoga we are discussing here. A fiery yogi is a highly spiritual individual — one who has established power over their lower nature, thoughts, and actions and who is on the path of continuous self-perfection and self-sacrificing service to humanity. Hence one can say the saints of all religions were fiery yogis.

Despite the fact that the term the *Fiery Experience* is modern enough and was first introduced by Helena Roerich to explain the way she received *Agni Yoga*, or the *Teaching of Living Ethics*, in the 20th century, it still was primary for the transmission of all the sacred scriptures known to humanity: from the Vedas and the Puranas to the Bible and the Quran. It was the Fiery Experience that lay at their foundation.

So the individuals destined to give people various Teachings of Light in oral or written form have been preparing for this through many lifetimes. In those incarnations they could have filled the role of priests, government officials, astrologers, or mere poets, but the main feature is their supreme level of spirituality. Sometimes they had to retire from their ordinary lives, moving into a pure realm far away from people and common vanities. They could also be called to the Chief Stronghold of Light, Shambhala, to restore their spiritual knowledge; and accounts of travelling to the East, to India, have been preserved in connection with many founders of philosophical and religious systems. Just before the transmission of Teachings, the representatives of the Hierarchy of Light worked with such chosen ones, purifying their bodies and souls, to prepare them to receive the supreme fiery energies that, without such training, might literally incinerate their physical bodies. Therefore, as a rule, these chosen ones were the Great Teachers themselves or their closest colleagues, who incarnated themselves amidst humanity for this inhuman mission. Usually, they were born as ordinary people, but in some cases, they could be high mediators.

After a certain period of time, when the selected disciples are ready, Teachers come to them in a dream or reality, often in the form of Angels, to convey through them Teachings destined for certain historical stages of development of various peoples, as well as the territories they inhabit. Such a transmission happens in a specific Ray of one of the Teachers, which represents a highly vibrational fiery stream, directed at the disciples' higher centres of consciousness.

There are Seven Rays, each of which is used to achieve certain evolutionary goals. For example, the Ray of Knowledge influences the brain centres. It is the Ray that protects and prevents new knowledge from distortion, serving as a special tool to translate the incomprehensible Cosmic Knowledge into what the disciple's consciousness is able to assimilate. However, it should be borne in mind that transmission in the Ray is not a dictation, but the *creative work* of the disciple. The Ray influences and awakens the corresponding higher energy centres, causing a strong influx of thoughts, images, and ideas, which the disciple then translates into words. That is, the disciple is in a high degree of consciousness, and creativity under the Ray can be called *divine inspiration*. And precisely because it is *creativity*, it is important for disciples to possess the talent that has been refined over the course of their numerous earthly incarnations. Thus, the disciples are the true co-authors of the Teachings along with their invisible Teachers.

During the oral or written transmission of Teachings, the crystallization of fires occurs at the level of the disciples' higher energy centres, which in turn saturate the whole surrounding world with new currents in the corresponding Ray. Thus, their centres emit already assimilated and processed higher energies into the world, which other people can then absorb, helping them start a new stage of their development. What then becomes public is only a part of the work produced by the disciples. The unpublished parts of the Teachings will be in the archives of Shambhala. Yet the most significant part of the unpublished work will be imprinted upon the entire space of the earthly world, from the lowest to the highest spheres. And all humankind on the planet will perceive the ideas of Teachings, regardless of the fact that they were initially given in particular languages for particular peoples.

However, each transmission of the Teaching of Light has its own individual characteristics, and therefore the above explanation of divine inspiration is provided only for general understanding. For example, many Teachings were originally given by the incarnated Great Teachers verbally, and significant periods of time could pass before they appeared in the form of sacred texts. In this case, those highly spiritual disciples were in the role of co-authors, who in their past lives were included in the inner circle of the Teachers giving the Teachings. Here, once the disciples had undergone special preparation, the Ray influenced their Chalice of accumulations, drawing out of it their memories of what the Teachers preached. And then the disciples creatively translated them into words in the appropriate languages and, at the same time, the crystallization of fires imbuing space also took place.

It is necessary to emphasize separately: no Teaching of Light can be given through mediumship, but any medium, given the appropriate steadfast aspiration, can become a mediator under the guidance of one of the Teachers and, subsequently, a fiery yogi.

THE GREAT MYSTERY
The Triune Teaching of Maitreya

ACCORDING TO PROPHECY, Maitreya's Teaching must precede His Advent. Thus, it was said that Three Teachings of His would be given in the West, the East, and the North.[1] Moreover, one of the drawings accompanying the recently found manuscript by Nostradamus, *Vaticinia Nostradami*, symbolically depicts Chakravartin, or the King of the Golden Wheel, whose Teaching was supposed to have been recorded by three women.[2]

The first disciple was Helena Blavatsky, who wrote her major work, *The Secret Doctrine*, under the guidance of the Lord Morya in the late 19th century in the countries of the West. As mentioned above, Morya is the Eldest and the Greatest of the Teachers, who in His essence is one with His Father, and for this reason *The Secret Doctrine* relates to the Triune Teaching of Maitreya.

Blavatsky was born the strongest type of medium, because of her special mission to convince humanity of the existence of the higher laws of Nature. But she is also the most striking example of the transfiguration of a medium into a fiery yogi. Following the yogic path in her previous lives, she succeeded with the help of her Teacher, Mahatma Morya, in becoming a high mediator and a fiery yogi in order to give *The Secret Doctrine* to the world. She began a new, hitherto unprecedented cycle of transmission of Secret Knowledge, which before that time could not be so broadly revealed to humanity, and was instead hidden behind hints in all sacred writings. She wrote her major work in the Rays of Lord Morya, who is the bearer of all Seven Rays, namely in the Ray of Knowledge and the Ray of Harmony through Conflict. It is commonly believed the Great Teachers entirely dictated *The*

Secret Doctrine to Helena Blavatsky, but in fact it was practically her own, fully fledged creative work in the Rays of Mahatma Morya. The "dictation" was limited mainly to the instructions and advice of the Teachers, through their letters, as to what sources she should use and what fields of esoteric knowledge she should cover.

As it always happens with true Messengers of Light, humanity did not accept Blavatsky and treated her like a charlatan, morally crucifying her by all available means, including fabrication of false evidence. All attempts to justify herself led only to even more violent disbelief on the part of her accusers and critics. But for a person who is under the constant influence of the Lord's Ray, it is extremely difficult to be among people in large cities, to be in front of a whole society. Unbearable pain and declining health, which was constantly exacerbated by the torments of both enemies and friends, resulted in Blavatsky's premature departure from the earthly plane.

The Secret Doctrine was significantly ahead of its time and later allowed such outstanding scientists as Thomas Edison,[3] Nikola Tesla,[4] and Albert Einstein[5] to make many scientific discoveries that have changed our world. Currently the works of Blavatsky, based on the most ancient texts stored in Shambhala, are especially valued by the highly spiritual lamas of Tibet, such as, for example, the 9th Panchen Lama[6] and the

14[7]th Dalai Lama. Thus, in her writings, she indicated that the climate change typical for periods of a shift in evolutionary cycles always results in earthquakes and other natural disasters.[8] And at the threshold of such a new cycle of evolution, a Teacher always comes to instruct a new humanity.[9] Yet at that time she could not specify exact periods, and therefore used the same enormous figures given in the scriptures.

Helena Blavatsky was required to sow in human minds the first seeds of knowledge about the Laws and Principles of the Universe, so as to prepare the soil, because the Cosmic Period was approaching when everyone, in their spirit, would have to make the most important decision of their earthly existence, choosing with whom to stand: with the Light or the darkness. The Hierarchy of Light has a rule saying that a chance is occasionally given twice, but never thrice. That is why the Hierarchy decided to give each human soul the maximum number of chances: the two Calls to Light that would sound through the following two Teachings.

It is Helena Blavatsky who laid the foundation for what was called the "Great Mystery" in *The Mahatma Letters* and could not be revealed in full to the understanding of humanity.[10] Even now this Mystery can be described and understood only on a primitive level. So, before the commencement of her work on *The Secret*

Doctrine, Blavatsky underwent special training under the supervision of her Teacher in Tibet. This Experience of the fiery transmutation of her body allowed the Teachers to prepare the way for the colleagues of Shambhala who followed, in order to continue and deepen this Experiment for the good of all humanity. Since the goal was to give the world the Triune Teaching of Maitreya during three sixty-year cycles, connecting Shambhala and the West, East, and North with a single thread, the prerequisite for this was the unification of the energy currents of all three female disciples, who were destined to reveal the Three Teachings to humanity. Simply speaking, their work had to involve elements energetically linking the previous Teaching with the new one, establishing spiritual continuity both invisibly and visibly, in the form of a particular piece of writing.

As we know from *The Mahatma Letters*, disciples who visit Shambhala, unless they are incarnated Teachers, cannot return to the world "completely," as it were. One of the principles of the sevenfold structure of their bodies must remain there, so as to form a *spatial fiery wire*, a secure connecting link for transmissions between Shambhala and the world, when the disciples return to their countries of residence. However, if disciples live high in the mountains, then there is no need to separate their principles, because the Teachers, if necessary, can freely descend to certain heights. Leaving behind one principle in Shambhala also allows them to save disciples who live most of their lives in the lowlands from fatal blows, especially at times when they are already on the verge of death. This is precisely what enabled the Teachers to intervene to save Blavatsky when she was on her deathbed, and accounts of her miraculous recoveries can be read in the reminiscences of her companions.

In esoteric philosophy, it is known that spiritual communication with one of the Teachers happens through a *single wire*, whereas communication with all the Teachers occurs through a *spatial wire*, which also gives access to the Ocean of Cosmic Knowledge. Since ancient times, sages have stated that all creations in the Universe are interconnected with each other by invisible threads, or rays, forming a light-bearing net. Hence, potentially, a single wire is available for every spirit, which is capable of connecting them not only with the Teachers, but even with Distant Worlds. However, in order to "activate" this wire and to connect with a Teacher, one must have enormous reserves of spiritual accumulations over numerous lives of self-sacrificing service to humanity, because this connection operates on the principle of a magnet: to receive something, one must already have something which is able to attract it. It is through these wires that the Rays of Teachers pass, affecting disciples' consciousness, and it is precisely the Rays that protect them, not letting anyone interfere in this process. As already mentioned, the preparation of disciples to receive the high-frequency energies conducted through the Rays is neither easy nor painless. Therefore, one should not identify these fiery wires with the channels of modern channellers, since the latter are protected neither from the intervention of any other forces, nor from the distortion of the transmitted information. Their quality and reliability vary significantly, in exactly the same way as any wired and wireless connections. Only if the channellers are highly moral and spiritual can their channel be protected, either by their own power or by that of the Forces of Light.

The single wire, then, has been used before in guiding the colleagues of Shambhala, who were to give the world various Teachings of Light. But the spatial wire, which allows the earthly disciples to communicate with all the Teachers of Shambhala, was first created during Blavatsky's lifetime. It becomes available only to fiery yogis at the higher degrees of spirituality, because it is much more difficult to use than a single wire. It requires significantly greater expenditure of energies, and thus has a much stronger effect on the disciple's health. Prior to this, the spatial wire was the prerogative of the Teachers alone. When Blavatsky left the earthly plane in 1891, this fiery thread that passed through the countries of the West remained in London, and the next colleague of Shambhala was supposed to arrive there, so as to "pick it up" and to continue the energy work, this time on new base currents. This is how, on the invisible plane, the unification of the fiery energies of previous and succeeding disciples takes place.

With this purpose, in 1920, as Helena Blavatsky had predicted,[11] the next disciple, Helena Roerich, arrived in London to begin recording *Agni Yoga* there under the guidance of Mahatma Morya, and then to continue it in Europe, the United States, and, finally, in the countries of the East, where she wrote the main part of her *Teaching of Living Ethics*. This series of books represents the path of fiery yoga, synthesizing all previous yogas, which was now formed for the first time as a spiritual practice available to everyone, and which serves for the transformation of all the bodies of the human structure. At that time, also, the first Call to Light began to sound, which is the energy saturating the entire space of the planet in order to attract consonant people by its magnetic power and thus to help everyone decide which side to stand on: the Light or the darkness.

In 1924, Morya was appointed the Lord of Shambhala. According to tradition, He was the 25th King of Shambhala, known as Rigden Dragpo and Kalki Rudra Chakrin. The appointment of Morya as a Ruler was associated with the commencement of the Era of Synthesis, and He, like His Father, is the bearer of all the Rays, or energies, given to the world throughout the history of earthly civilization. Therefore, during the ceremony of enthronement, He took the Name of Maitreya as a tribute to His Father, the Teacher of Teachers, who Himself would soon be manifested on the planet. After all, the Advent of Maitreya began in 1942, a date which, for certain reasons, was obscured in the scriptures — yet some researchers succeeded in understanding that the giant figures were merely symbols, and they widely declared as much to the population of India in the 1930s.[12] At that time, He was indeed, for the first time in thousands of years, incarnated in Shambhala at the level of the Supreme Spheres of the planet, obtaining single wholeness with His Eldest Son, Morya. So, in other words, the Solar Hierarch fully manifested Himself in Morya at the hour when Morya took the Name of the Lord of Shambhala, Maitreya.

During the period from 1920 to 1955, the Teachers under the guidance of the Lord of Shambhala were able to conduct a unique Fiery Experiment together with Helena Roerich. Previously, many had approached it, and the closest was Sri Aurobindo, but still the conditions of his life were unsuitable. This Experiment was needed because, as ancient Teachings warned, the strongest fiery energies, coming from the Cosmos, were to affect the whole Earth and humanity starting in 1999. However, the spiritual level of earthlings was not high enough to pass this period painlessly: the devastating future for the end of the 20th century, which Edgar Cayce saw and predicted, was a *reality*. And to prevent this and change the destiny of humanity, Roerich agreed to give herself over to the test of the spatial Fire — those very cosmic energies, which soon were to reach the Earth.

For the first time the Fiery Experience was held not in reclusion, but among people in the conditions of everyday life: while Roerich travelled across the East, and then in the towns of India at the foot of the Himalayas. The pure natural environment of the mountains, and the loving people all around, were a great help in conducting the unprecedented Experiment with Roerich. Under the close supervision of her Teacher, the Greatest Lord of Shambhala, she passed through the opening and transmutation of *all* energy centres, perceiving all Light available on the Earth, that is, all the Seven Rays. Thus, for the first time, an earthly person could communicate not only with all the Teachers, each of whom has His Ray, as was possible for Blavatsky, but with all other members of the Brotherhood, between whom the Seven Rays are divided by tonality. This was necessary because the task was to conduct a huge number of experiments on Roerich's human matter, and the entire Brotherhood needed a way to communicate with her directly. It should be noted that communication even with one Teacher demands incredible tension in the higher centres of the disciple's consciousness, which not every mediator, even one at a very high level, is able to withstand. But thanks to her spiritual achievements, Roerich had both wires: one to converse with the Lord Morya and the other to communicate with the entire Brotherhood, which also gave her access to everything that was happening in Shambhala.

In normal earthly conditions, the process of opening and transmutation of energy centres is excruciating and agonizing, because their highly vibrational nature does not correspond to the low vibrations of the earthly environment. This process must be conducted only under the supervision of a Teacher, and cannot be made on one's own, and even more so in the conditions of modern life. Roerich was often ill for a long time, since her body could not withstand such fiery tension, and even communicating with the people closest to her was painful. Only for certain stages of the Experience did she need to retire to places high in the mountains, but even there the Teacher rescued her from fiery death.

As a result of this Heroic Deed, all seven bodies of her human structure were developed and transfigured, whereas Roerich's consciousness had reached the superhuman level. Conscious and creative Cosmic Co-operation and Construction together with the Great Lord of Shambhala had become available to her on all the seven planes of Existence. The vibrations of the Cosmic Co-operation are so high that they cannot be perceived and comprehended by the physical brain without its destruction. It is an indescribably difficult state, and the fiery overstrain would often disable her for long weeks, when she was forbidden not only to write or read, but even to *think*, in order to restore her strength. However, Cosmic Co-operation is especially efficient when the individual is in a purified physical body that helps to accelerate not only the evolution of the Earth but also that of the Solar System.

Thus, Roerich could travel in her mental body together with other members of the Brotherhood within the Solar System, carrying out the assignments of the Lord. This may all seem strange and fabulous to ordinary people, who are accustomed to the need for huge spaceships for travel through the Universe. But in Tibet, there are special closed monasteries, where monks practise travelling first within our planet and then also on other planets; this is all possible for the human spirit, and it must be said that such mental flights were also available to Nikola Tesla. During the Cosmic Co-operation, Roerich also could provide assistance to both individual people and the entire Earth, such as, for example, participation in battles with the dark forces, containment of the elements, and the extinguishing of the underground fire.

Along with the opening of her centres and co-operation with the Brotherhood, Roerich was writing *Agni Yoga* in the Rays of the Lord of Shambhala that essentially reflects her own path of transformation of all bodies, which now every aspirant can follow. The recording of the books occurred in the Ray of Knowledge with the further projection on the Ray of Love-Wisdom. Every day of hers was full of intense creative activity: she spent from morning till late at night writing down conversations with her Teacher, preparing new books of the Teaching for publication, translating them, and carrying on an extensive correspondence with her numerous correspondents from all over the world, including President Franklin

Roosevelt, who partially accepted the advice given by the Lord of Shambhala.[13] However, far from all of her work was published in printed form. While her major work, describing all the effects of the Rays and her body's reaction to them during the Fiery Experience, is yet to be evaluated by humanity, that, too, will help new scientists make incredible discoveries.

Moreover, Helena Roerich translated *The Secret Doctrine* into Russian. This, up till now, is the only and the most correct translation, as it was carried out in the same Rays in which Helena Blavatsky worked. Nevertheless, this work was necessary not only in view of the need for a translation of this fundamental masterpiece, synthesizing all the previous Teachings of Light, but also in order to unite the energy currents of Blavatsky and Roerich on an invisible level, as occurred during the translation work.

The main component of Roerich's Fiery Experience was the assimilation of the new Rays coming from the Cosmos. Such assimilation of the Rays, unknown to the planet, by the heart of an incarnated earthly woman, like an experienced doctor testing new vaccines, enabled the Teachers to gradually inoculate the majority of humanity with their formula, so that in the future these energies would not produce unexpected alchemical reactions in human bodies and, as a consequence, in the planetary body, causing catastrophes on a global scale. So, thanks to this sacrificial Heroic Deed, the Teachers succeeded in averting the devastating scenario predicted for the end of the 20th century. Roerich's Experiment allowed the current generation of humanity to almost painlessly inhale the new fiery energies now enveloping the whole Earth and to reduce the number of natural disasters to the minimum level permitted by the Karma of humanity. It should be noted that it is the inability of humanity to fulfil the primary commandment given in all the Teachings of Light — to love — which causes disasters, including a catastrophe on a planetary scale threatened in the late 20th century. Because only the energy of Love, a high level of spirituality, enables one to absorb new energies.

By the end of her life, Roerich had reached the highest level of spirituality and enlightenment possible on the Earth. She laid the foundation for a new phase of human development. And it is also thanks to the hearts which responded to the first Call of the Lord of Shambhala, which has been resounding since 1920, that the Fire has been able to penetrate earthly spheres, become assimilated as a wider flow, and direct the destinies of entire continents into a positive course.

Helena Roerich foresaw that soon many beautiful mediators would appear on the Earth, who would help accelerate the spiritual awakening of humanity.[14] And a year before her departure, she warned that the Fiery

Experience would be continued by the next disciple at the end of the 20th century.[15] After all, her Experiment, as Helena Blavatsky's had previously done, had provided an opportunity for the Teachers to form entirely new matter for the next colleagues of Shambhala preparing for earthly incarnations.

In 1992, this permitted the beginning of the Fiery Experience of Zinovia Dushkova under the guidance of the Lord Maitreya on a new level, first repeating everything that Roerich had passed through. Thus, Dushkova underwent the same agonizing process of opening and transmuting energy centres in the conditions of ordinary life. She experiences the same constant pains of the physical body, which vary only from unbearable to bearable. But in present conditions this is aggravated by the fact that she has become a hostage of technical progress, because, to maintain experimental integrity, the disciple must live the same life as other people do. Whereas during the Fiery Experience it is undesirable to have contact with, for example, computers, due to their harmful radiation. At the same time, without them, it is impossible to work on writing and publishing new books, or indeed to lead a modern life in general. However, this also serves as a kind of experiment for the Brotherhood to find ways to minimize the harm from technical progress. Ultimately, all existing technologies, no matter how advanced, are only imperfect duplicates of the abilities of the human spirit.

So, during the first three years, the Teachers were systematically working with certain of Dushkova's energy centres, an activity that was accompanied by terrible pains and fever lasting for months. And then, just before she started writing books and making records necessary for spatial work with the Brotherhood, the unification of the currents of hearts began. This process, for convenience, may be called the vision and hearing of the heart, because both symbols and multi-level pictures on a gigantic scale were manifesting along with the intersection of all Times — the past, present, and future — and all this was accompanied by the silent music of the spheres, in whose basis was laid the rhythm of Fire. The entire infinite Ocean of Wisdom appeared before the gaze of the disciple's heart, but any attempt to pour into human words even a drop of it was accompanied by suffering, owing to the awareness of the impossibility of doing so. Only then did she realize that all recorded words were only a key, which opens this Infinity to all seeking hearts.

In 1995, it was necessary for Dushkova to go to India so as to "pick up" the fiery thread Roerich "left" amidst the Himalayas, but now she was to bring it predominantly to the countries of the North, the Slavic lands. In her case, as previously with Roerich's translation of Blavatsky's *The Secret Doctrine*, the energy and vibrational unification of her currents with the currents of Roerich took place in the course of her work on the book *Brotherhood: The Empyreal Abode* from 1995 to 1997, during which a tuning of spiritual strings and consonance occurred, much as in music. This volume, written mainly in the same Ray in which Roerich worked on *Brotherhood*,[16] is a kind of unifying bridge between *Agni Yoga* and *The Teaching of the Heart*, between the first and second Call, affirming succession not only on a spiritual level, but also in the form of a book, before the next cycle of work in a new Ray.

Thus, Dushkova, just like Roerich, also has both the single wire to converse with her Master and the spatial one for communication with the whole Brotherhood, so that it is possible to monitor the progress of her Fiery Experience. In space, these wires look like invisible and scintillating fiery-silver threads of Light connecting the hearts of all the participants in the Experiment. While working, when they conduct highly vibrational energies from the Teachers, one can imagine that a straight fiery line goes from Shambhala to the disciple, travelling around the world, and, along this line, space is especially intensively saturated with positive and constructive energy.

Nevertheless, there is a difference between how a Teaching is given and how the disciple's communication with the Teachers occurs. For instance, the message of one Teacher or another appears as a superluminous little star in space, which bears a particular colour and which then unfolds into a "letter of instruction" before the gaze of the disciple's heart, depending which country she is in and what labour she needs to do. In addition, the approach of the High Spirits to the disciple is accompanied by the subtlest aroma, unique to them. And it must be said the disciple can easily discern the attempted approach of dark entities in the very beginning, since it is attended by dark dots or a kind of dirty "plasmoids" that carry a foul stench.

Zinovia Dushkova was working on *The Teaching of the Heart* in co-operation with the Lord Maitreya from 1997 to 1998. Precisely since 1997, the last and final Call of the Lord of Shambhala has been resounding throughout the entire space of the planet. And the appearance of this Teaching in Russia at the end of the 20th century was predicted by such famous seers as Mitar Tarabich,[17] Edgar Cayce,[18] and Vanga.[19]

Maitreya is called the "Great Heart," His Era is the Era of the Heart, and therefore His last Teaching is entirely dedicated to the awakening and transfiguration of the human heart. The heart, being the focus of Light, is the supreme organ of cognition; its invisible radiation operates over both short and long distances, and is capable of changing space. It is in the heart that all the possibilities of the future are laid — the whole divine potential of each human being — and humanity must come to its realization through the heart alone.

Dushkova wrote the book series *The Teaching of the Heart* in the three cycles of manifestation of the Ray of Love-Wisdom while travelling in India, Egypt, Israel, and Japan, but mainly in Russia. This Ray was manifested in full measure for the first time on the planet.

Recording in the Ray of Love-Wisdom places the most intense strain on the energy centre of the heart, which, like no other, can imbue space with currents already assimilated. Therefore, work in this Ray entirely depends upon the state of perception of the disciple's heart and on the sounding height of the heart's crystal, called *Ringse*, which the disciple has attained. The disciples must achieve the level when their consciousness is moved into the heart. This is due to the fact that the human Divine Self is contained therein, as is mentioned in all scriptures. In esoteric philosophy, it is considered that the Divine Self, the seed of the human spirit, is a particle of the Cosmic Father, one of the Seven Teachers, which was begotten in His Rays at the very beginning of the Grand Cycle of Evolution. It is according to this principle of "cosmic kinship" that disciples find their Teachers when they are ready.

In this way, once Dushkova has shifted her consciousness in the heart, she can merge it with the consciousness of her Father, the Teacher, and thereby gain access to Infinity. Meanwhile, the Ray of Love-Wisdom emanating from the Heart of the Teacher and directed into the heart of the disciple seems to uncover an endless source of inspiration: thoughts and ideas pour out as a continuous flow, which she then consciously and creatively translates into human words. However, unlike the writing done in the Ray of Knowledge, the disciple does not hear the voice of the Teacher as such, but it is the Voice of the Heart, also called the *Voice of the Silence* in esoteric philosophy, in which everything in the Universe speaks. Therefore, it can be said that the Teaching was transmitted from the Heart to the heart, and for this reason, naturally, it is entirely intended for human *hearts*, not minds.

It should be noted that the Voice of the Silence also takes the form of a sacred language, known as Senzar. It is the primordial language from which all other tongues have originated throughout the development of humanity. The language of Senzar has a traditional form of speech and writing, familiar to us, but with its own specific rules; it also has higher levels which are substantially different from our understanding. It is these levels that are the closest to the Voice of the Silence. So, at the higher degrees of consciousness, the disciple's eye of the heart can "behold" the Voice of the Silence as the synthesis of fiery signs and the geometry of certain manifestations of rays, which is also characteristic for conversations in Senzar between the colleagues of Shambhala, taking place on the subconscious level. When, for example, the Teachers speak in Senzar with people who do not know this language, they will have the sense that the Teachers are speaking in an unknown tongue, but at the same time, they will understand everything perfectly.

Now, for the first time, Zinovia Dushkova was to write the main part of her books in the Rays of the Lord through the Fiery Experience not in pure mountain conditions — but in the midst of human masses in the cities of the world populated by many millions. This is because of the fact that a large part of humanity lives in the lowlands, in big cities, and they cannot all physically be moved to the mountains in order to assimilate new energies. The atmosphere of cities is so poisoned by the negative energy which the imperfect thoughts of millions of human consciousnesses emit that fiery energies cannot pass through it in their pure form without the presence of the magnetic attraction of highly spiritual hearts within that territory. Yet when they combine with this poisoned human energy, they cause unexpected reactions in organisms, manifesting in the form of various diseases. This complicates the process of the Fiery Baptism, which Helena Roerich was the first to undergo in earthly conditions and which now the whole of humanity is passing through.

In every city of the world, there is an invisible point which bears the greatest concentration of negative energy, cemented by people's evil thoughts. During the writing of the Teaching, the Ray of the Lord must pierce this layer from the outside, while the disciple simultaneously must break through it from the inside. The disciple should, through the division of the spirit, consciously, so to say, separate into several hypostases to make the breach of this stratum possible. It is incredibly difficult in the poisoned environment, and advanced monks and yogis practise this solely in pure, natural conditions. After all, it is unbearable to have open centres in city conditions, but it is necessary during the work. There is an enormous load upon the disciple and her heart, and often her energy centres are intoxicated, and inflammation may occur, which leads to fiery death. It is a giant risk; several times the Lords of Light had to interfere to save Dushkova. Nevertheless, the successful accomplishment of such a task allows her to let the Fire through into the lowest points, illuminating and healing this space. And the majority of people living within this territory are now capable of perceiving new currents without significant negative consequences for themselves.

Every heart which has consciously accepted Maitreya's Call of the Heart is able to heal the space around it in the same way, receiving and assimilating fiery energies. Thus, everyone, taking in a particle of the work produced by all the Forces of Light, is able to build a new beautiful pattern of the future for their city, country, and continent. After all, it is only when people themselves apply 50% of the effort that the Forces of Light have the right to intervene in order to help. In other cases, unfortunately, humanity must drink what it has brewed for itself; otherwise, it will learn nothing.

While Zinovia Dushkova is writing books amidst the crowds, the Brotherhood closely watches her, monitoring the reaction of her energy centres and her internal organs on a cellular level. But in such moments, people who approach the disciple also become participants in the Fiery Experience. The thing is that the places where she is making records, both during and after the process, begin to attract, like a magnet, an unusually high number of people. Therefore, their reaction is monitored as well, in order to know how they respond to different doses of the "irradiation" passing through the disciple. All this then allows the Teachers to find the necessary ingredients in the laboratories of the Brotherhood to improve the functioning of physical bodies, providing assistance to all of humanity. Their observation also covers the representatives of the Mineral and Vegetable Kingdoms, which almost instantly react to the vital currents the disciple emits, as well as the Animal Kingdom.

In addition, just like human beings, the planet Earth, too, has energy centres. Since ancient times, the Initiated have often erected temples on these powerful sites. And they embedded special magnets in their foundations. As a rule, they tend to attract a great many people. In esoteric philosophy, such places are called *Points of Life*, and may be associated with certain planets and constellations. Points of Life can also be formed by objects imbued with the highest energy, which were created by or belonged to the Great Teachers when they were incarnated as human beings. Typically, these Points formed by sacred objects are located in large museums around the world, and when the objects are moved, the Points move, too. Some of the planet's Points of Life were dormant, but in the late 20th century, the time came for them to awake, in order to saturate those areas where they are located with positive and constructive energy. It was also necessary to transfer those that were already active to a new level of sound, corresponding to the current stage of evolution. Therefore, Dushkova wrote *The Teaching of the Heart*, as well as all her subsequent works, not only at the lowest points, but also at these Points of Life located in different countries, because they can be awakened or transferred to a new qualitative level only by the touching and influence of the Ray passing through a physically incarnated person.

Since Dushkova, just like Blavatsky, spends most of her life in the lowlands, there is an occasional need for her to thoroughly isolate herself from the world and spend some time in the heights. This is because a disciple who has achieved a certain level of spirituality cannot remain long in the poisoned atmosphere of the cities, and must often move away into Nature. For instance, it is known that Jesus Christ, Gautama Buddha, and other Great Teachers frequently went to the desert or mountains to restore their strength, which was rapidly exhausted when in contact with people, and it could even lead to their premature death. This is what happened, for example, with such disciples as Blavatsky, Ramakrishna, and Swami Vivekananda. It is also known that when Mahatmas Morya and Koot Hoomi appeared briefly among people in the 19th century to carry out certain orders of the Brotherhood, they had to be in complete solitude and isolation for a few weeks or months afterwards so as to recover their strength, so dirty and poisoned was the environment in which the majority of humankind lived.

However, Dushkova's need for isolation is also connected with the permanent change of the fiery energies coming from the Cosmos and, therefore, all her books must reflect these phases of their changes on the energetic level. In this way, before starting to write any of her major works, she is always required to move high into the mountains for some time, so that the Teacher can prepare her heart and body for new fiery currents. This enables the harmonious crystallization of these energies in their pure form at the level of her heart, which then can receive their modified states in lowlands conditions and radiate them outwards, already in the assimilated form, saturating space.

It should be said Zinovia Dushkova does not make notes on her Fiery Experience, describing her feelings and reactions under the influence of certain Rays, because Helena Roerich had already done all of that. All her writings which do not form the basis of new books are focused only on the spatial work, and therefore they are destroyed immediately after completion. Only a small part of the recommendations given by the Teachers remains, which may someday be published in the form of a sequel to *The Mahatma Letters*.

In remote times, the sacred writings were written anonymously, and the names of the authors of many of them are still unknown. After all, even if we take the Gospels of the Bible, which carry the names of the Apostles, not all of them were written personally by them; some were written by their unknown disciples. However, we now live in the modern global world, where there must be a person responsible for each creation, whether it is an author, musician, or inventor. Moreover, an anonymous work, being in the public domain and without protection, quickly becomes distorted. Thus, when the first Russian edition of *The Teaching of the Heart* was anonymous, people began to ascribe its authorship to others, and during publication some distortions crept into the text. Similarly, some people started to re-issue Dushkova's other anonymous books, complementing them with their own prefaces and claiming to be their authors. Seeing that these things harm the Teaching and in this way people may distort it, she has begun to designate herself as author in order to protect the text for which she is responsible.

The Teaching of the Heart and other books by Zinovia Dushkova are only a small portion of the fruits of the work she is accomplishing. As already mentioned, all recorded words are only keys for those who are able to read between the lines, to see beyond what is written and to penetrate to a deeper sense with their hearts. However, a significant part of the daily work done during the Fiery Experience, lasting for almost 25 years on the border between life and death, is spatial and invisible, something that envelops the whole world and cannot be described. The healing of space, the work with the energy maps of various lands — each new day brings more complex tasks in the service of humanity. Her heart is continuously receiving ever new currents and the constantly increasing intensity of the Fire, which, in transmuted form, all the Kingdoms of Nature — from the Mineral to the Supreme Spiritual — can now imbibe. Daily work with the Brotherhood is being carried out to find new formulas of matter for the future developmental stages of humankind. And the Cosmic Co-operation with the Solar Hierarch occurs consciously on the seven planes of Existence, later transitioning to twelve duodecimal layers; and here the creative Cosmic Construction now relates *not only* to the evolution of the Earth and the Solar System... — which, of course, is far beyond the limits of human comprehension.

THE MYSTERY OF LIGHT
The Advent of the Messiah

BLAVATSKY, ROERICH, AND DUSHKOVA composed the Triune Teaching of Maitreya before His Advent, which paved the way from intellectual knowledge to the wisdom of the heart, being bound by an indissoluble energy thread with Shambhala through the West, East, and North over the course of three Eastern centuries. But how is this Coming supposed to happen?

The legends that have been preserved in various religions say each Saviour of the World was immaculately conceived by the Supreme God or Holy Spirit. According to esoteric philosophy, there is Truth in this, which can be explained in the following way. A High Spirit, acting as a Father, projects His Ray onto one of the energy centres of the future Mother and thus an immaculate conception takes place. Usually this Ray and the corresponding centre represent the energy dominating in space in that historical period. Then the Father's Power gradually flows into the Son. So, for example, the conception by the first energy centre can be connected with Zoroaster. The birth of Jesus Christ happened in the Ray of the Orange Solar Flame, as a Solar Logos, which is connected with the second centre. Krishna and Buddha represent the third centre. At each stage of evolution, there is the highest level of such a birth. We live in the Fourth Round of Evolution and, consequently, the conception and birth of the Supreme Spirit must occur through the fourth energy centre — the heart.

In esoteric philosophy, conception and birth through the heart is called the *Third Fire*. It is characteristic for civilizations of the highest spiritual development, such as, for example, Sirius, the homeland of the Solar Hierarch. In earthly conditions, one can imagine that a man and a woman create the Third Fire by the fire of their love, begetting it in the heart of the supreme level of the mother's sevenfold structure, as though in her aura. Then, if the fire of love of this couple has not abated, the Third Fire is conceived within the mother's heart on every level, which may last up to seven years. When the Fire is established on all seven planes, including the physical, an invisible fiery fœtus appears, within which a luminous and angelic creature is born. In this way, he may be carried in the heart of his mother for up to twelve years. And then, if this spirit considers it appropriate, he may be born on the physical plane; if not, he will depart for the higher worlds as an Angel, Archangel, or Planetary Spirit.

The Advent of Maitreya should take place on the Earth in a similar way. Our planet is the lowest point of His descent in the Solar System. All the planets in the System are inhabited, and the fact that we cannot see their dwellers through our physical and imperfect devices does not mean they do not exist. Other civilizations of the Solar System, belonging to the category of sacred planets, are simply at higher levels of development, which do not involve evolution in physical bodies. His incarnations on each of the planets are because of the fact that the whole Solar System needs to begin a new stage of its development. Thus, He transmits the giant current of Fire from the Supreme Divine Worlds, which in turn gives an energy impulse for a new cycle of ascent of humanity on one planet or another.

According to Cosmic Laws, each planet belongs to the humanity populating it, and He can manifest Himself on it in all His Fiery Glory only when summoned by its dwellers. After all, the expression of free will is an inalienable Cosmic Right of every creature, and therefore the Forces of Light conscientiously honour it, and they never impose anything against the free will of humanity. By a particular time, an answer about whether people await Him appears on the pans of the Cosmic Scales, a decision — *yes* or *no* — taken consciously or unconsciously by every heart. If *yes* prevails, He is born in the Highest Image characteristic of that planet; if *no*, then He goes higher after accomplishing His invisible Mission. It should be noted that He has already been incarnated on all other inhabited planets, and none of them answered *no*.

It should happen exactly the same way on the Earth: if *yes* prevails in the hearts of humanity, He will appear in the flesh. But, as noted above, it cannot be a physical body, something humanity's decision deprived Him of two thousand years ago. The Cosmic Laws entitle Maitreya to be born in the heart, which, from the perspective of the Cosmos, is already the physical world of the Earth and the flesh of mortal man, but at the same time it will not pose discomfort to that part of humanity which does not await Him. Moreover, it is clear that if He were to be incarnated as an ordinary man, then society would again deride Him, "holy" priests, quoting the Bible, would call Him the Antichrist or the false messiah, and eventually the same fate would await Him as that endured by Jesus Christ. This must not be allowed, and if humanity committed this crime for a second time, it would be punished according to the full severity and justice of the Laws of the Cosmos. That is why the Advent must take place in the Spirit with the transmission of divine energies from the Heart to hearts.

From esoteric philosophy we know that, after the death of His physical body, Jesus Christ managed to transform its matter on an atomic level in such a way as to essentially resurrect it, thereby making it immortal. But it was the densified subtle body, the so-called Body of Light, which could become temporarily visible to the eyes of those who were pure in heart. Therefore, the Resurrected Christ would suddenly appear before His disciples and would disappear just as unexpectedly. The Fiery Transfiguration of Christ has been a supreme achievement on the Earth. And it is the one that has created that formula of matter which will compose the Body of the Coming Messiah. Besides, over the millennia, those who are Initiated into this Mystery of Light have taken part in further energy improvements in His

THE MYSTERY OF LIGHT

Light-bearing Matter, which, while not physical, may become visible to highly spiritual people.

Now let us find out where He will come from? The answer to this question was given long ago in the sacred Puranas: the Kalki Avatar will be born in Shambhala.[20] Then, in the 16th century, the famous Korean astronomer Nam Sa-go left prophecies from a mountain-dwelling sage. They predicted that the King of Kings would be born north of the 38th parallel and that He would come "from the mountain of the island nation."[21] Indeed, the 38th parallel runs through the Pamirs, which, together with the Himalayas, form the "Roof of the World," where legends often place Shambhala, also known as the White Island. In the 19th century, Blavatsky confirmed that it was in Shambhala that the Messiah expected by all religions would be born.[22]

Throughout the history of humanity, Shambhala has received a great many names, all of which were revealed to different peoples according to the capacity of their consciousness. Thus in the Christian tradition, it is believed that Christ ascended into *Heavenly Jerusalem*. This is the symbolic name of Shambhala, the Kingdom of God both on the Earth and in the Heavens. In this way, as described in Acts 1:11, the Resurrected Christ will indeed return from the Heavenly Jerusalem "in like manner as ye have seen Him go into Heaven," but now in immeasurably increased Power and Glory.

Each Lord of Light has a date marking the highest manifestation of His Rays associated with certain flows of cosmic energies. Thus, as mentioned in the beginning, in ancient Egypt, people knew that the Day of the Sun God Ra was 19 July, since it was connected with the manifestation of the rays of Sirius, and they even celebrated the New Year on this day. Therefore, all the major stages of His Coming to the Earth are invariably related to this sacred date. Moreover, the well-known prophecy of Nostradamus speaks of "the seventh month" — i.e., July. Also, in 1989 the still unexplained phenomenon of the "Salsk Celestial Code" told people that Christ would return on exactly 19 July.[23]

According to Buddhist scriptures, before the impending Advent of the King of the Golden Wheel into the world, a sacred flower, the *udumbara*, appears, which blooms once every three thousand years.[24] It was in 1997, when the Great Lord of Shambhala, Maitreya, filled the entire space of the planet with the Message about the forthcoming descent of the Messiah in the Image of His Son and started giving His Teaching, that the first appearance of this celestial flower was noticed on the statue of Buddha in a temple in South Korea. Its blossoming also preceded the "entrance of the Messiah" in 1998 predicted by Edgar Cayce,[25] when His Spirit was begotten in the aura of His earthly Mother. It should be borne in mind that the advancement of

Maitreya the Messiah towards the physical spheres of the Earth consisted of several main phases, about which more can be found in *The Book of Secret Wisdom*.[26] But now let us look at the last and decisive stage.

In May 2005, in another temple in South Korea, the celestial udumbara flower bloomed for the second time, signifying that on 19 July 2005 the Messiah of all times and peoples descended from Shambhala into the material world of the Earth, being born in the heart of His Mother. The impulse of the mightiest Fire occurred in the area of the sacred Mount Kailash and lasted 24 days. The giant energy waves which accompanied the descent of the Messiah manifested themselves through the full power of the forces of Nature: on the same day there could be the strongest heat and the strongest cold, along with such a manifestation of the elements that even grass in the Himalayas was charred.

But one should not be confused by the fact that the Solar Hierarch is simultaneously in multiple worlds: He is on each of the planets in the Solar System, manifested as the Lord of Shambhala on the Earth, and at the same time was also born in the heart of His earthly Mother as the Messiah. The Divine Spirit, who has reached the supreme level of evolution, possesses the quality of *divisibility* that lets Him act in full consciousness on different planes of Existence through the manifestation of His Hypostases.

THE GREATEST TEACHER AND HIS TEACHING

The sacrament of the birth of Gods on the Earth will always remain a mystery extremely difficult for human understanding to fathom, for only God can give life to a God. The Father has to be consubstantial with His Son, and in order to achieve this, the Solar Spirit first has to appear on the Earth, so as to then reflect Himself in the Image of His Son — the Solar Messiah — who is now His full incarnation on the Earth, rather than the partial incarnations that appeared before.

For twelve years, up until 19 July 2017, He, being within the heart of His Mother, will have been transpiercing the planet with the most powerful fiery energies. Thanks to these energies, the human structure of those who have preserved the purity of their souls will change in the near future. And the impulse that He will have been giving for twelve years will be sufficient for inevitable changes to begin in all spheres of life, step by step lifting all of humanity to a new, more spiritual stage of its evolution.

As described above in connection with the Third Fire, on 19 July 2017 He will be born at a higher level, in the Subtle World, as a Planetary Spirit, so as to begin returning gradually into His own World from there. His Teaching will remain on the Earth, showing everyone the only possible way — the Path of the Heart. By the Cosmic Right, any Earth-dweller, being initiated by the vibrations of His Rays, if ready, will be able to become His disciple and start to follow the Path He indicated. And to be a disciple of Maitreya means to transform oneself and to become the embodiment of Love and Compassion; and true disciples will always be able to hear their Teacher through their hearts.

Also be aware that in the Higher Worlds there is nothing like the earthly understanding of *Time*, and that is why we can assert that, from the earthly point of view, He will be in the Subtle Spheres closest to the Earth for thousands of years.

If the call of earthly hearts is strong enough to form a *yes* on the Cosmic Scales, He will receive the Right to manifest Himself in a "physical" body in the material world, too. This depends upon each person and may happen at any moment, "for ye know neither the day nor the hour." If the call of humanity comes during our lifetime, from the perspective of Cosmic Justice, a Mystery of Light will occur. Thus, while the mercy of Christ forgave people two thousand years ago, the Mother still lost Her Son. And humanity is called upon to return Him to His Mother by its positive answer in the age in which She lost Christ. But again, though He will be visible to "physical" eyes, He will not have the same body as all people; it will be the "Glorious Body" in which Christ was resurrected and in which He afterwards appeared before the Apostles. His appearance on the Earth in such an Image will bring an even greater, unprecedented amount of Light and fiery energies, which will accelerate a thousandfold the ascent of both the planet and all humankind. In addition, when such a giant Spirit as the Messiah is manifested on the Earth, His Power of Love will impel the planetary body towards a state of balance, which will harmonize all currents, and the enormous disasters caused by people themselves will be no more — that is, this will significantly pay off the Karma of humanity that it created during this cycle of its evolution. But whether humanity wants all this is something everyone must decide for themselves.

The date of 2017 is important, because everything in the Universe is subject to the Cosmic Periods, which, being special combinations of rays and position of stars and planets, determine timeframes for the manifestations of particular events. And so, if this Period is missed, it will never happen again. Yet it was indicated in the Bible long ago. Many researchers have done calculations on the basis of the Bible and announced the importance of this date as the year of the possible Second Coming of Christ.[27] We can only supplement it with the prophecy taken from *Maitreyavyakarana*:

> "Maitreya, the best of men, will then leave the Tushita heavens, and go for his last rebirth into the womb of that woman. For ten whole

months she will carry about his radiant body. ... He, supreme among men, will emerge from her right side, as the sun shines forth when it has prevailed over a bank of clouds."[28]

"And there appeared a great wonder in heaven; a woman clothed with the sun, and the moon under her feet, and upon her head a crown of twelve stars. And she being with child cried, travailing in birth, and pained to be delivered."[29]

All sacred texts have seven levels of understanding. In order to understand these quotations in the context of the Time of Advent, one needs to read them using an astrological key. In September 2017, there will be a unique arrangement of the celestial bodies, with the Moon, Jupiter, Mercury, Mars, Venus, and Regulus aligned; the Moon will be "under the feet" of the constellation of Virgo, "clothed with" the Sun, and the nine stars of Leo together with three planets (Mercury, Mars, and Venus) will form the "crown of twelve stars." Since ancient times, the planet Jupiter, the King of Planets, has been a planetary symbol of the Messiah, while Regulus, the King of Stars, is His stellar symbol. Thus, symbolically, the King of Kings will descend from the "Tushita heavens" through the aligned planets into the "womb" of Virgo, being represented as Jupiter, which will enter her "womb" for 42 weeks, or almost ten months. In other words, it appears that the Nativity of the Messiah in the year 2017 in the Heavens was symbolically described long ago in the sacred texts.

Similar findings indicating the significance of the year 2017 have also been discovered in the geometrical construction of the Great Pyramids in Egypt.[30] Moreover, Rabbi Judah Ben Samuel, a legendary Jewish mystic of the 12th century, after making his own biblical calculations and astrological observations, predicted that the Messianic time would begin after the 10th Jubilee year, which concludes in 2017.[31]

Concerning the Jubilee year, there is another famous 19th-century prediction made by Ellen White, a co-organizer of the Seventh-Day Adventist Church. In her vision, she saw the Second Coming of Christ in the year when the Jubilee would commence. Initially, her followers have combined several events into one and come up with the year 1844, which naturally did not justify their hopes. However, modern researchers looking into her prediction and the Bible interpret it to mean that this "Jubilee" must be a Sabbatical Jubilee, coinciding with the day of purification of the Heavenly Sanctuary, and fall on a Sunday. Their calculations have found only one possible date that meets these criteria — 22 October 2017.[32]

THE MYSTERY OF LIGHT

Now let us turn to Muslim prophecies. It is known that the Imam Mahdi, the Islamic Saviour, was initially identified with the Prophet Isa, or Jesus Christ. Only later, with time, people began to perceive the Mahdi as an independent image. As a saying of Muhammad states,[33] the Mahdi will emerge in the years 1420–1439 of the Islamic calendar, equivalent to the period of 1999–2017. It is interesting to note that the Islamic new year of 1439 falls on 22 September 2017 of the Gregorian calendar, a date which accurately coincides with the Bible's Cosmic Event destined to occur on 20–23 September 2017. Furthermore, researchers of the Quran broadly use a numerological key: each letter of any language has a numerical value, and when researchers apply it to certain verses of sacred texts, they can determine specific dates of future events. Thus, it has been found that the Quran's verse concerning the return of Jesus Christ[34] yields the number 1439,[35] which, if taken as denoting an Islamic year, again points to the year 2017.

Nevertheless, it should also be added that, despite the fact that researchers have calculated specific earthly dates for the possible Coming of Christ, they still cannot pinpoint the actual Day of Epiphany, as it depends upon human will alone. That is why it is absolutely impossible to tell when, exactly, humanity will be ready for it — it could be in the coming years, decades, or centuries. But, that said, all indications point to the year 2017 as the correct Year of Nativity, although, as we already know, it will happen in the Subtle World, in the Heavens, from where He can descend at any time in the same way He ascended there two thousand years ago.

For those who may misunderstand the significance of the year 2017, it is worth mentioning that there will be *no* "end of the world" with apocalyptic pictures. Everyone will simply make their Final Choice in favour of the Light or the darkness through accepting or rejecting the Messianic Fire. The Period of Choice has lasted since 19 July 1999, which is again discussed in detail in *The Book of Secret Wisdom*, but there is still a considerable mass of "sleeping" humanity that needs to make a particular decision before 19 July 2017. By this date, all of humanity will have made its Final Choice in spirit, whether or not people are aware of this. And then, according to their deeds throughout all of their earthly lives, everyone will gradually take their deserved and appropriate place on the Ladder of Evolution and in the Solar System. That is, every person will pronounce a "sentence" on themselves, which is essentially what constitutes the Last Judgement in all religions. But again, this *will not* be manifested in any global catastrophes.

In relation to the Last Judgement, it is interesting to recall the famous prophecy of St. Malachy about the last Pope. In 2013, it was on everyone's lips, when Pope Benedict XVI suddenly abdicated and Pope Francis was elected. According to this prophecy, Francis is destined to be Pope during the Last Judgement and the Second Coming of Christ.[36]

The acceleration of time is also an indication that humanity is now facing a decisive choice, since the Age of Maitreya is the age of acceleration in everything. Thus, the Bible says that "days shall be shortened"[37] before the Advent, and one of the sayings of Muhammad indicates the acceleration of time as a sign of the approaching Judgement Day.[38] And currently, despite the fact that days and nights still contain 24 hours, many people around the world have a feeling that time is quickening, it is moving much faster than ever before. However, the speeding-up of the pace of modern life is also conditioned by new technologies. Many high spirits are now specifically incarnated as scientists so that, through technology, humanity can be accustomed to the speed and tension of the Higher Spheres, where almost everything happens instantly, where there is no concept of *Time* in the earthly sense. So, for example, mobile communications and the Internet, which enable us to easily contact people we wish to speak with or to get instant access to knowledge we need, are only primitive duplicates of the fiery wires and spatial Treasury of Knowledge described here. Therefore, as the spiritual level of humanity gradually increases and as people realize the potential of their hearts, our need for technology will fall away.

As the supreme and supernatural sign of the approaching Advent of the Lord of Light, the appearance of the sacred udumbara flower is now to be found all over the world; it blossoms in the most unexpected places;[39] it sometimes emerges out of nowhere, filling space with its aroma, and in the same way suddenly vanishes into nowhere.

The predictions of all the great prophets have already been fulfilled in detail. Every day we observe anomalous manifestations of Nature, now in one corner of the world, now in another. And regarding climate change, new temperature records have been set in almost all countries of the world and the average temperature on the planet increases with every new year.[40] At the same time, it is reported that the number of natural disasters occurring annually has increased tenfold in comparison with the 1950s.[41] This all suggests that we are the contemporaries of a change in the cycles of human evolution and, accordingly, we are at the threshold of the epiphany of the World Teacher.

Yet the most eloquent sign of the Great Advent is that more and more people around the world are intuitively feeling that it might happen even during their lifetime. American surveys, for example, confirm that the number of adult residents of the United States who are convinced that they will witness the Second Coming of Christ in the near future, has increased from 24% in 1997 to 41% in 2010.[42]

However, whether the long-awaited Advent will take place in our physical world or not, whether it will happen during our lifetime or whether only future generations will be worthy of beholding the Messiah — all this now depends upon everyone's choice and upon the collective will of all the inhabitants of the planet Earth, since this cannot happen against human will. That is why this Event is broadly announced as a last chance, so that everyone can consciously, and by their free will, determine whether they accept or reject the Messiah in their hearts.

In conclusion, it is worth remembering that even old traditions say the Advent of the Messiah is, first of all, the conscious acceptance of His Teaching, for thus the Supreme Wisdom and Divine Power will be incarnated not only in one single individual, but in all awakened hearts, which indeed will create a New Heaven and a New Earth.

APPEAL TO HUMANITY

I AM AN IMMORTAL SPIRIT, watching you from the snow-white summits of the Sacred Himalayas. As such, I am appealing to you, dwellers of the New World.

I call upon you to expand more broadly all your limiting frames of vision and to encompass in your thought the entire beauty and vastness of the Great Ocean of Infinity. Do not restrict yourselves to the narrow confines of dogmatism, as I, being known to many peoples, each of whom name Me in their own way, have called you to profound religious tolerance.

You have traversed a long and unusually difficult path, having tempered your hearts by the feats of your life. Do not think all the trials are over, for the darkness is still strong in your lands, and it is far too early to sheathe the sword of the warrior and hang it on the wall. Your armour must not be allowed to gather dust in museums, but used to protect you from the spear targeted at the very *heart*. Hastily arm yourselves at the hour of the Commander-in-Chief of the Shambhala Army's descent into the world.

The last battle which takes place on the Earth determines the destiny of the whole Human Race. To be or not to be a protector of the planet, to link one's own destiny with the Divine Fire or not — this is a question each human heart must answer for itself. And whoever decides to *be* will stay; yet those who say *no* will quit the field of battle forever. And the warriors who win the final Victory over evil will lay down their weapons and heavy armour. The planet will no longer know the darkness, for she will be altogether flooded with the Light.

Respond to My final Call, and merge your hearts in a flaming prayer for our planet — our own dear Mother. "Help the Earth!" — the servants of Sacred Love are ringing all the bells and summoning the Heavenly Host. Let us strike the final blow at the enemy through the openness of our hearts, harbouring no hatred towards the defeated. They who are covered with the Shield of Love know no failure, whereas those deprived of Her presence will always be vulnerable. I offer each of you a shield and urge you to array yourselves in the Armour of Love — thus will you triumph!

Compose hymns to the One who is descending to you from the High Mountains, so as to establish the Victory of Light on the Earth. Know that the Gift of the Empyreal World will be with you for ages eternal.

I have given you My Teaching, protected as it is by the Shield of Love, and have proclaimed the Victory of Light which is destined for the holy lands. Accept the Gift of the Hearts which behold with great Love the New World as it regenerates in the Divine Fire. All of Our highest hopes are centred on you, children of the long-suffering world. And may each word that comes down from the Empyreal Heights resound within your hearts as a mighty ringing bell, calling you to Sacred Love.

The Saviour is coming! He will sanctify the entire Earth with Divine Fires, and this Light will be enough to illuminate the whole Universe.

Accept My Message about the descent of the Lord on the eve of the Holy Annunciation, and may Love, our Supreme Creator, bless you all!

Maitreya
24 March 1997

THE CALL OF THE HEART

India — Russia
1997

PART I

India

Kalimpong
5 October

The Call of the Heart reaches the summits of the human spirit.

I gave you My first Message, sanctified by the Name of Morya.

I am giving you the second Message:

Go with the Name of Maitreya,

Create in the Name of Maitreya,

And thus will come the Kingdom of Eternal Light.

I have spoken.

M.

6 October

I am your Heart.
I am your Battle full of the Light of Love.
I am your boundless Heaven.
I am your morning Prayer directed to the Sun.
I am the Rainbow of Love,
I am the Word of Beauty,
I am the Ethereal Eternity!

"From where do Messengers come?"
"From the Valley of Infinite Dreams."

"From where is a Song born?"
"From My bottomless treasures."

"Where do rivers flow, washing the fallen with their waters?"
"To the One Source that brought forth the murmur of melodious waters."

"Who is capable of perceiving the Song of Maitreya?"
"The joyful heart!"

I am singing a hymn to the heart, offering it a treasure.
I speak from Heart to heart:
Accept My Call.

PART I

7 October

I glorify the Lady of All Creation.

Her radiance illuminates the leaves of My Garden.

Cross not the borderline of anger and cast not yourself off from Her Face.

Leaves assemble well when wind cannot scatter them.

Each leaf of knowledge must rest on good soil, fading in their weightless whirl, full of light.

Then I shall tell you a lot, when you pacify the running of your thoughts, absorbed into the vortex of the fallen leaves covered with decay.

Darken not your light which streams from the depths of the heart grateful to Me.

Drop not the banner which crowns the way of victory.

I shall touch you with My Wing, and Maya will recede temporally, but you should take care that illusions do not delude you forever.

Not for the sake of crowds do I give, but for seeking hearts.

I am not bringing Myself, but I wish to bring your flaming heart, brimming with Love, to the throne of the Lady of All Creation.

I said: You will enter My World by the Name of the Ineffable One.

8 October

Aspire to enter the flow of waters when it is full of the might of fresh streams.

Do not lose a moment, for it is capable of developing into the Eternity of Love, but do not turn it into endless suffering.

I shall gather gems, raising luminous pearls from the depths of the sea.

You will need only to string them on your own thread, placing them in a beautiful line.

Adorn yourself, My disciple.

It does not befit you to be apparelled in rags, finding amusement in the false glitter of stones.

A leaf of My Garden is imbued with the eternal current nursed along by Love.

Ages remember the Name of Maitreya: He grows His Garden by the Power of Love alone.

You will meet Me everywhere and follow Me, provided you are thirsting for Love.

She is the only one I have; She fills My treasuries.

Love closes the lips, impressing a seal of silence on the one who loves.

PART I

Love is not a loquacious babbler — she is a bird frozen in flight; she is a string stretched taut over an abyss.

Emit a sound and revive the bird of Eternity.

Tune your lyre to a delicate sound, allowing it to pour out all of your pain and deathly anguish.

Let it die away, melting before the Face of Immortal Love just as wax melts before the fire which sears it.

Like the Sun, I shall go from one edge to the other, illuminating your hearts.

Following My footsteps, flowers will spring up, exuding the aroma of Divine Love.

I shall spread My Garden within the human breast exhausted by the pain of despair.

May the Light of Love be forever!

Darjeeling
9 October

Book I
Joy

My Joy is My legacy for everyone.

The fiery heart cannot live without its currents, for then it would not be able to serve the Fire.

Was not it with Joy that My Pilgrim went forth, bearing the bloody cross of this world?

Is it not you — you who hammered the rude cross for the followers of the Supreme Spirit — whom I caressed by the currents of Joy so that you might burn the gloomy snares entangling your heart?

Come to Me, the humiliated one, ascend to Me, the fallen one — and you will experience the currents of Divine Joy.

We do not judge, so you must not pass judgement on Our Joy, for you know nothing about it.
Its sacred currents are accessible to the fiery heart alone.

I have spoken about the heartfelt Joy that led Us through the darkness of life towards the destined Light.
It nourished Shulamith and the great heart of Solomon, who paid for Joy at the cost of his beloved's life.

The cost of Joy is high.
But one who has paid will not lose that for which one has paid in full.

And Akbar, searching for his Shulamith all his life, appealed for Joy, at the same time sorrowing deeply in his heart.
And the light of a distant Star would not leave him during his earthly path, affording him generous currents of Joy.

PART I

It is not easy for Our Pilgrim to bear the cross of Joy.

And Shulamith bends under the burden of sorrow.

But He who has brought Light to the world has ordained us to reach the Eternal Source by Joy.

Covered with wounds, the heart sings, dedicating the great Song of Heroic Deeds to Maitreya.

And people's hearts lit up in response, anticipating the great Joy.

The Joy of Maitreya is coming, filling earthly sources.

A generous stream will bring a pearl to every heart.

And great Joy will begin to shine, revealing all its fiery facets to the world.

Follow the path of Sacred Joy, thereby multiplying the Light of the Fiery World.

You will ascend by Joy!

Book II
Fortress of Love

I protect those who love with a shield and encircle them with the walls of a fortress, making it impregnable.

Everyone who approaches these walls with a weapon sowing death will be thrown back.

Let your spirit grow stronger within the walls of My Towers.

And at the midnight hour do not open the gates, which would only make your fortress accessible to your enemy.

I protect with the Shield of Love, arming you with a single piece of equipment.

Love — this is your Shield and My Fiery Sword.

Fight valiantly, maintaining the resplendence of a smile on your lips.

My warrior will triumph by Love!

Severe were the faces of My warriors, but they covered their enemies with the kindness of their hearts.

And so they would never know defeat of the spirit.

I commanded My warrior to show pride: be proud, My knight, of your Fiery Country and illumine with the Flame of Heroic Deeds the path amidst the thick of the battle, as manifested throughout the world.

You are invincible as long as you hold the Banner of My World and Peace in your hands.

PART I

Do not let the flame fade away within your breast: it nourishes the heart, showing the focus of Light, whereto I can send a ray of My Love.

Be like a lamp, burning before My Face.

And ascend as a fiery star.

There are no barriers in your way, for they were burnt by the increased flame of your Love.

I know the only way: it is woven by Love!

Dawn will rise over the world, drawing the exalted flame from the depths of human hearts.

You know the Book of Sacrifice.

Sacrifice a particle of your heartfelt light and give it to your enemy.

They will be transfigured merely by a single current of Fiery Love.

My Fortress is high, and the walls of My orderly Towers do not separate Me from you, but you yourselves wished to stay out of My Temple.

For one who aspires to Me there are no impregnable walls, for they are woven with the Flame of My Love.

But your fortress is more solid than stone.

Why do you separate yourselves from Me, when you know the omnipotence of My Fire?

The walls of My Fortress are the currents washing with the Fire.

Enter the limits of My Love — they are limitless.

I know the fiery word, bearing the seal of might.

And now I present it to you: Love!

As if by a magic key, it will open all the closed gates for you, and all the walls which before were impregnable will fall beneath your feet.

I have opened the Gates of Mystery and told you the Truth.

And My last Word will tell you of the Heart.

I am your Heart.

Book III
The Heart

My Law is the same for all: to love!

There is no Love beyond the heart, there is no Fire beyond the loving breast.

The mind does not know the nectar of Love — only the heart may know it.

I shall always be with you, as long as you open wide the gates and let Me into your heart which is yearning for Love.

PART I

I shall always hear your call, if you have already accepted My Call.

The trembling of your heart reaches the peaks of My Sacred Mountains.

The Abode of Eternal Snows is full of the crystallized currents of your Love.

The Himalayas will piously preserve the gift of grateful hearts and, multiplying the light of treasures, will return them to you, increasing them by a thousandfold.

I am not aflame only where there is no Me.

You multiply Love by the Name of Maitreya.
You serve the Light by the Name of Maitreya.
You acquire omnipotence throughout all the worlds by His Name.

I have said: Love!
I shall say: Give life to that which is covered by the decay of death, reviving it by the Flame of My Love, which is generously pouring into your heart.

I shall tell you about Love more than others, for My time has come: the Time of Love that is timeless and limitless within the periods allotted to her by the Great Plan of Divine Evolution.

The Flame of Love is immortal!

Solomon knows this.

The Great Pilgrim carried his earthly cross, having only once come to know the currents scorching with fire within the earthly spheres.

Shulamith alone had the key to his flaming heart.

She left, having poured the warmth of Love upon him.

But he had been searching for her during all the millennia of his earthly existence.

Perceive Divine Love, you who are called by Me, touching the currents of Love outpouring through the heart of My Shulamith, who returned to the world so as to endow it with Love for the last time before departing into Eternity, to the feet of Our beloved Mother.

I shall generously bestow Gifts upon you, but throw any bestial grin into the Fire and adorn your contemptuously pursed lips with the Light of My smile.

If you have chosen My Path, go with joy, protecting with the Shield of Love your heart, which loves the whole world.

Know Love, both mundane and supermundane, for only one who has experienced the entire warmth of the incinerating flame will be capable of perceiving Divine and Fiery Love.

PART I

I shall tell you of the heart, but only of that heart which is brimming over with Love.

I shall tell you of Love, but only of that Love which abides within the heart.

And trust My Word, too, if you possess the heart.

I have said: Love!

Let her be thrice blessed in your heart, which is beloved by Me!

Yes! Yes! Yes!

The end of the trilogy recorded in the Abode of Darjeeling amidst the currents of the Sacred Himalayas, encircling the whole world with the Shield of Love.

Calcutta
12 October

The leaves of Maitreya's Garden will fall off at the appropriate time, and good soil will accept them into its womb, so as to return them again after processing to the magnificent crown.

My leaves are immortal.

Whatever happens, I give you a single commandment: Love!

Love will compose a new pattern in exchange for the broken one and will breathe in fresh currents, compelling you to advance rapidly towards a distant goal.

Understand yourself correctly: there is no other path either great or small.
You are making your own way within yourself.
And every step leads to victory.

The leaves fall off at the time of a battle and at the time of reaping.
Every leaf bears My Word, full of Love.
Only by this exalted sign will you distinguish My Word from all the other sounds produced by life.

Look forward, for bridges have already fallen behind you.
Why would you go back when the goal is shining ahead?
Freeze in time when you have to look back so that time does not turn backwards for you.

I believe in the future of the Human Kingdom, and that is why I am shedding leaves so generously.
I feed them to My children, arming them with Wise Knowledge.

Step into the future together with Me.
Sow the seeds of Love.

PART I

And they will grow as a wonderful Garden, multiplying their leaves in time.

Know the flowering Time of Love!

Allahabad
14 October

I shall not call your life a crime, if you have fulfilled My work, and have brought light into the darkness surrounding you.

A gloomy life should be given away to gloom, because I have ordained for you only the Light of Love.

The past cannot be resurrected: it is dead.

To be like a necromancer does not befit you.

You bear the triumph of Life.

Look into the future; it is there that your goal awaits you.

It is difficult for Me to express My feelings: there are few vessels ready to accommodate the currents of My Heart.

You are proceeding with such great difficulty because you keep your empty vessels closed, unaware of all-overflowing Love.

I shall tell My warriors the Word of Love.

I shall give them the scrolls of My gathered Knowledge to read.

I shall show them the way to the Fiery Sanctuary: Enter and serve your dream, whose name is Divine Love.

A leaf drawn to a leaf composes a magnificent crown.
Dry branches fall off in time, all by themselves.
My Teaching does not know death.

I come at midnight and shine for you at noon.
I am always with you, but you must manage to accept the obvious, and I shall dwell in your heart forever.

I form the cup of your patience.
Every moment of earthly life can multiply the treasure.
Recognize My signs and put them into your treasury like pure pearls.
And may their light be inextinguishable.
Gather them for the ages, and remember this: by enriching yourself, you also endow passers-by.
I sing about the generosity of My warriors, composing a hymn to their boundlessly multiplied patience.

PART I

Naggar
17 October

To My friend and My enemy I just have one thing to say: show patience.

It is impossible to mount the scaffold of the earthly glory without it, and without it, it is all the more impossible to experience the Ethereal Glory — the Fiery Glory.

Love herself will go around the world, blessing with the wing of Joy.

Rejoice in Eternal Love!

I shall let My pearl guide your footsteps.

Lift up this sign of My Wisdom; it will save the lives of many.

Give Me a chance to enter your heart and fill it with My Gifts.

I bring Love, wishing to fill the entire world with her.

The Creator produces a Song, weaving it from the currents of life, regardless of the state of the soul.

Sing the Song of Heroic Deeds — and your heart will grow stronger.

I freeze in running, as though a full-flowing cloud had spread over the withered and thirsty soil.

Take a drink from My Source and quench your thirst for ages.

I shall come down from Heaven, stepping straight into your hearts.

I shall bring them the light of Joy.

Take care to prepare a place for My currents: in them lies your salvation.

18 October

I have commanded the Path of Love, but not everyone has heard it with their heart.

Those who listen with their ears cannot hear My Voice and do not accept My Word, for their hearts are deaf.

I prolong life for those who strive for it.

Death has no power over My warrior.

Immortality is the lot of everyone who comes to Me.

In the early stages of life, look forward with optimism and fill the days of your future with dreams.

But shine especially brightly at the moment of sunset, thereby affirming a new picture of life that will unfold beyond the borders of the material world.

PART I

I pacify a storm, taming the gusts of wind which strive to break you.

But you, too, make efforts to set up new sails and to restore the broken masts at the proper time.

I shall not let you be absorbed in the gloomy abyss.

I shall rise as a Star in front of you and I shall guide you in the way.

Aspire towards the goal.

I shall dwell in hearts till the end of time and will not forsake My warrior in the dark.

And I shall offer you Knowledge and Love — with them you will measure your steps to the stars.

I shall leave the house, where there is no heartfelt warmth, and I shall never approach thrice the one who chases away the Light of My Heart.

Those who have chosen the darkness have no place in My House.

Only those who have yearned for Light will abide under My roof.

They will build new nests, rearing little nestlings of their own.

And their wings will grow stronger from the Flame of My Love, and they will illuminate the whole world with fiery flares.

New people are coming!

Welcome them with your heart.

19 October

We overcome the path within ourselves.

Armageddon takes place inside of us, and a victorious march is ordained for the spirit of light.

You will win if you hold tight the Banner of Love in your hands.

The borderlines of the ages are being erased, and man is becoming capable of peering not only into his present day, but also into his future.

How long will it take to become a creator, when one transcends Time which limits the vision of the heart?

The New Man will live in a new Earthly House.

Give yourself the opportunity to spread wide your wings.

I urge you to look more boldly into the day of tomorrow.

You will be a witness to the New World, and will be delighted with the manifest Plan of the Lords.

Sufferings will end, because you will be filled with Love.

Her supreme currents will supersede everything dissonant and affirm the Light of unprecedented clarity.

Nothing will approach the Fire nor extinguish the bright Flame.

PART I

You will acquire unprecedented power: the power over yourself.

I shall hand you a sceptre, but do not let the rod of power confuse your mind, for thereby you will sacrifice yourself.

You will be endowed with unlimited power to sacrifice, but only to sacrifice yourself.

Herein lies the Truth of Love.

I shall come again, if you call Me; but if you reject My Gifts, you will not be able to approach Me; and to one who has distanced oneself — My path will be long.

To get closer to Me is within your power alone — but I am always close by.

Anyone who wishes to find the Path of Salvation must be willing to go together with Me.

We shall proceed not by reasoning, but by the unified aspiration of the heart, which beholds the goal crystal-clear.

Like a hot and all-consuming flame, your spirit will pass across the earth and will rise as a fiery star.

Tread the clear path, according to My fiery signs.

I have said: The Heart!

It will show you the way.

20 October

You are advancing with the Name of Maitreya, illuminating the perishable world by your bright step.

May the seal of Love be imprinted upon all your deeds, and thus will you become the personification of My World.

I do not call twice one who refuses to go.

My Call resounds for new people only.

Go in peace, with My Name — and you will reach Me.

I shall be eternally within your heart if you have perceived the Call of Eternity and responded to the silent prayer of My Heart.

I am indivisible with you.

We constitute a single whole Principle.

And our bonds are indissoluble for ages eternal.

Leaves fall off at the proper time, heralding the approach of the winter cold.

For many, a severe testing time is coming.

And who will be covered with the ice of oblivion depends upon the manifested spirit.

But new leaves spring up, and My Garden gains an unprecedented magnificence.

I conceal high aspiration within Me.

And do not turn your face to look into the dark abyss.

PART I

Keep the bright purpose before your gaze — only thus will you ascend towards the Fire.

But those open wide to gloom will indeed come thereto, for their goal will dissolve in the darkness.

I shall march across bright expanses when My victorious Army banishes all fierce anger.

I am leading My warriors, cleaving by the Sword of Love all the barriers encountered on their way.

You will triumph through Love! — I affirm.

The storm on the sea of life will abate, and the sounds of battle will be muffled throughout the unembraceable expanses.

Peace and calm will be established on the Earth.

Love will spread her wings and will rule the world eternally.

I present a leaf from My Garden to each and everyone.

It is brimming with Love, for it is imbued with My all-loving current, and its shape resembles a heart, tied with the crown of My Tree by a silver thread.

"Love the world, love the Light!" I remind you through every fallen leaf.

Grow Love infinitely and change your leafage with the seasons, revealing the ever more luxuriant crown of your tree.

Delhi
21 October

Warriors came to Me by dint of their feats of arms; however, only those reached My Gates who had been self-sacrificing and did not fight for their own glory, but in the name of the triumph for the justice of the Light on the Earth.

I told the warrior what the goal was: Victory in the name of Love.

I shall pass the sceptre of power to the hands of the one who has comprehended the sacrifice of the path and has not refused to go further, every hour sacrificing the most precious in one's life.

Power is — sacrifice.

It is human destinies that are entangled, and threads are interwoven into indissoluble knots.

But the Sword of Maitreya is raised over the world, and a single fiery stroke is enough to free many from the fetters of slavery.

A leaf falls at your feet: some will pick it up, and some will grind it into the dirt, pressing it deep into the ground with their heel.

My leaf will return to Me, demonstrating the maturity of emerald colours once the dust is shaken off.

PART I

But the one who pressed it down with their heel I shall not see in My Garden, for their ashes will be incinerated by the Fire.

I do not threaten, but tell the truth: everyone prepares their own lot.

Many are subject to the Periods.

Both animals and birds take a step forward.

But humanity must make room for them and take a step up the rungs of Evolution.

Do not mix with wild beasts, but abide with winged creatures.

Do not I wish to see you amidst Angels and Gods praised in hymns?

Yes, indeed, among them, My children!

And that is why I am toiling incessantly.

Understand My labour, but understand it with your hearts.

Again and again I have attempted to ignite your hearts.

Rarely have We encountered on Our way those who are eternally on fire.

But We fanned the sparks We encountered by the warm flame, and out of them have arisen stars of the first magnitude.

They became the first and led others into the starry sky, illuming them as a bright example.

I ordain fiery and selfless devotion for you, My children.

22 October

Do not grieve prematurely when you look at the chaos around you.

I am weaving light-bearing patterns that will appear at the appropriate times.

Similarly, a leaf will not fall before the time, until it is ready to tear itself away from the treetop and carry out its own flight.

Before any long flight, direct all your thoughts towards a single goal, so as not to be driven by changeable winds.

Know your purpose and follow it by the most direct path.

I shall help you reach the Divine World, if you yourself aspire to walk with Me.

We shall merge with a unified stream, and it will carry us on wavecrests into stellar expanses permeated by the Light of Love.

Everyone will reach it, and no one will fall behind in the way if their heart has accepted Maitreya as their Leader.

PART I

And stars never fade, for, breathing out the Fire, they are simply preparing to breathe in more deeply than before.

And their fiery might increases by generous giving.

I would like to see each of you as a star.

As you share My Light with others, you will thereby multiply your own fiery power.

Accept My Gift with your heart: I offer you My Garden.

Enter with confidence and you will find there everything you had lost along your way.

Peace and calm will occupy your heart, and the currents of Love will melt the weight of your earthly burden.

Think about how you can improve your life.

Might it be too dependent upon someone else's will?

May the will of Heaven merge together with your own will!

Only thus will your achieve liberation.

I have given you many commands, however, they can all be combined into one word, namely: *Love*.

Only one who loves will be able to fulfil all the commandments of Heaven.

Love unites them all into a single Law.

And this way you will observe faithfully the prescribed Charter.

Love is your goal.

23 October

I shall enter your heart and shall soothe the outbursts of anger directed towards My child.

I shall not allow the darkness to celebrate any victory over your body, for the seal of My Love will save you from many troubles.

The dark power will be no more, know this and advance towards the victory destined for you.

Man is woven together by a single Law, and therefore must be filled by unified currents of Love.

You cannot come into conflict with yourself and produce a schism.

Everything must be one and whole in this world.

Will scattered cells be able to carry the seed of life, if separated from the fabric of the whole?

Only by merging together can they represent a single whole organism capable of living.

Reconsider your way and agree with the promptings of your heart.

PART I

It knows the best solution, for it holds counsel only with Me — provided, of course, that it is permeated with the currents of Love.

Each evening, make it a rule to look back on your day and to summarize the deeds you have left behind.

Look through the prism of Fire and try to see everything through the eyes of the Teacher.

Only in this way will you be able to catch a shadow that has inadvertently slipped in.

And do not let it pass into your future day, but bring forth the boundary of Flame, giving anything good over to the will of Fire — not only that, but also anything that could cast a gloomy shadow over your life.

We are building together our Temple of Love.

We are erecting walls on the foundation laid by the High Spirits before us.

And we shall crown the dome in accordance with the stellar periods.

Nothing will force us to cancel the construction, and the grin of the darkness will be powerless to shake our faith that the Temple will be erected.

The Temple of Love is My Fiery Song, but all the worlds will catch onto it.

I bestow power upon everyone: you are omnipotent when you are brimming with the currents of Love, for My treasures are open to those who absorb My Fire in order to endow the whole world with it.

I wish to see each of you as My co-regent.

Remember this.

Aspire to this.

New people will come and they will bring everything new in place of everything decrepit.

The entire world thirsts for renewal, tired of the stench of forms corrupted by decay.

I am advancing together with the new people.

Do not overlook the Light of Salvation, which has been glistening upon your path.

Listen especially ardently and look especially closely at everything new — perhaps, you will be able to sense My sign in that.

Every instant I am bringing Fiery Renewal to the world.

Know about this.

Puttaparthi
26 October

The aspiration towards the Light is praiseworthy when it is accompanied by a desire for the transfiguration of your own inner world.

PART I

However, if you have not purified your inner self, how is it possible to begin cleansing others, looking as you do through the prism of your own dirt?

Start with yourself, O man.

Do not think that We want to make idols of Ourselves when we urge you keep the image of the Teacher before you every hour.

Not for Ourselves do We care, but for you.

And if you hold on to the image, you will always be protected.

I serve Truth and Love.

Form the rungs of your ladder from the same composition.

The ladder of ascent is high, and other matter is not suitable for deposition in the higher layers.

Rejoice at the labour I have called you to in the name of Divine Love.

The psaltery has frozen, and cold has penetrated human hearts.

Why have sounds frozen on your lips?

Is it not because the darkness has deepened?

But you know that the darkness is especially fearsome just before dawn.

Do not be frightened by ghostly shadows that will be dissolved with the first chords emitted by the solar light.

Conceal not your own light, thereby you will multiply the marvellous sounds conveying the Beauty of Life.

Light — Colour — Sound — here is the Truth which is being presented to you!

Give yourself your word: to utter as few words as possible.

Do you not know that you immensely exhaust yourself through unnecessary verbal extravagance?

Save your strength, as each grain might be of benefit both to you and your neighbour as the gift of salvation which comes at the edge of the abyss.

Silence will strengthen the heart.

It is sad to watch that cold of speculation which humanity is dissipating every hour: dirty grey flashes are swirling, exuding the stench of a bad odour.

Did not I give you an abundance of beautiful thoughts whereby to illumine your mind?

A life-buoy ring is thrown to everyone, but it is your task to hold onto it and save yourself.

Do not let yourself give in to the illusion of hopelessness and drown.

Do not immerse yourself in a gloomy vortex, O you who bear the light in your heart.

Sadness is not for you.

Joy is ordained for you.

PART I

27 October

You will tell Me that it is painful for you to bear your cross amidst those who reject the gift of your Love.

I shall not condemn those who have thrown off their heavy burdens, but I shall help in every possible way those who are ready to continue their path with such backbreaking burdens.

I shall loosen the belts which leave a trail of blood, and I shall not let them pierce the body with new force.

Heavy is the cross, bitter is the burden, but you must not break under it, but bring it to the Source of the Eternal Fire in order to drop it in the all-consuming Flame.

Give food to the Fire.

I know a lot and I keep silence about many things, hiding the patterns of Flame until the time appointed.

Periods are foreordained for everything, and no one can violate them — either on the Earth or in Heaven.

A seed will germinate at the appointed hour, and a reaper will come to fetch a tight spikelet — but no earlier than the fruit ripens.

Autumn is for gathering harvest, but the sowing must be done in spring — be aware of the celestial signs pertaining thereto.

Allow time for the maturing of your thoughts and do not hasten to make thoughtless, premature decisions.

Thought itself will be able to take shape in action if it acquires sufficient maturity, and is filled with the juice of an all-creating force.

I am calling upon you to think big and beautifully.

But remember that in the world there is nothing more powerful than the currents of Love — and so I ask you to imbue all your thoughts with the vibrations of Love.

You will be able to cope with yourself if you call upon Me for help.

Often you do not know with whom you are fighting an invisible battle when you are attacked by an entire demonic host of mercenaries.

You fiercely strike your enemy by My Name, as though by a good solid staff.

And may the words of Love slipping off your tongue interlace like the links of luminous chain armour, which is capable of protecting My child from the enemy's spear.

Arm yourself ardently, summoning all the might of My Love to yourself.

For those who go along with Me, victory is guaranteed.

PART I

Merge with your thoughts, at every moment and at every hour thinking about Love alone.

Find the luminous strength within yourself to appreciate and love every thing that bears life.

Always look for a reason to justify, but not to accuse and condemn.

Follow the path of a bright thought.

All the celestial servants are weaving the luminous threads of destinies, but people are trying to paint the entire "yarn" in gloomy tones.

Why murmur against fate, when white thread takes on other colours in dirty hands?

I call for purification, and that is why I am pouring the all-cleansing Fire upon the Earth in order to bring all the filth to naught.

But throughout eternity the threads woven from Fire can never be stained — remember this.

It is sweet to sleep, but awaking is inevitable.

All the bells have struck midnight, and the time has come to herald the noon.

The Banner of Peace is raised high.

The New Age, without delay, is marching with a broad step, illuming ever new spheres of life with its Light.

The Sun of Maitreya has been ignited.

Joy has shone on the path.

Advance towards the Light of My Heart, I am ready to embosom everyone directed towards My World.

28 October

I rejoice when you rejoice.

Imperceptibly merging into a unified current, we multiply bright forces, offering a splash of fires to the spheres surrounding us.

We are able to enrich the world, but we can also make it poor, depriving it of life-affirming currents.

You possess wealth — the light of your smile; so share it with the world so that it becomes richer with Fires.

Dissipate the dark and establish the Light with great Joy.

Flowers do not bloom on ice floes, and so the petals of smiles will never grace the faces of the bearers of gloom.

But in the dark soil the roots grow up which nourish the flowers to be revealed to the world.

Throw a seed into the utter darkness, and a shoot of Light will rise towards the Sun — the Heart of Maitreya.

Give your enemy your brightest smile.

PART I

The noise will fade away, and you will hear the melody of your heart — it will resound distinctly, rising above all the other voices of the world.

What could be more important than the sounds produced by loving hearts?

The many-voiced choir will blend into one melody, composing a single hymn — praise to the Exalted Creator who has imbued the world with the flow of Love.

A pure phrase will harden on your lips when you understand your inability to comprehend it.

And do not say a word, foreseeing the reaction of your interlocutor in advance.

Sound, like a pearl, must find its place in a single harmonic line.

But to cast pearls under the feet of those who trample upon them — has long been determined to be a completely pointless task.

You will achieve much more by silence.

People are — Gods!

This is known to every leaf growing on the Tree of My Garden.

Gods are immortal, but man is mortal.

How to reconcile these contradictory concepts?

I shall say one thing: when you cast off your clothing, do you identify yourself with the outworn cloth and die?

Similarly, you can cast off your body, like an old waistcoat, as it can no longer contain your spirit that has miraculously grown up.

The spirit is — immortal!

And it is absolutely worthless to grieve over a piece of outworn clothing.

Gods are directed into the future and throughout eternity never experience nostalgia for the past.

Lips will close, eyelids will shut, hands will fold, as the earthly work is completed, and feet will grow cold as they approach the final boundary.

A perishable body cannot step over the edge of the circle outlined by Life.

But the spirit will indeed step over, spreading wide its flaming wings.

It knows the one and only entrance and in an instant will bring you to the Gates of Eternity.

There you will find the Light and peace for your soul, but do not tarry long amidst the caressing currents of Fire.

Remember that the world is groaning in unbearable pain.

Hurry to come back again, stretching taut the luminous thread which serves as a living artery of Fire for anyone languishing in the gloom.

I shall meet you in the Ethereal World, but only to remind you that I am already waiting for you in the earthly world.

Bear the cup of patience with a measured dignity — any abrupt splashes may cause it to lose its valuable contents.

Not to empty the vessel have you come into this world, but to return, after filling it up, and rise several rungs higher.

I had already told you of patience before, but you are having difficulty assimilating the truths which have been revealed to you for immediate use.

By patience alone you must build the bridge which will lift you up to Me.

29 October

New thoughts will come to you, bringing new opportunities for the growth of the spirit.

Listen to yourself and find those sounds of salvation that lead to the liberation from the fetters of old ideas with their annoying sounds.

Accept a new thought as a life-buoy ring thrown by My Hand.

Trust not barking dogs: today they bark at your enemies, and tomorrow they will be ready to bark at you as well, if you do not toss them a piece of bread in time.

As long as they can bark, it is not important for them whom they bark at.

All character traits are formed in the maternal womb, crystallizing in a certain formula that will dictate certain norms of behaviour.

And it seems that the fœtus has its own character, for it dictates its terms while still in the mother's womb.

But one cannot consider the beginning of the generative process only from the point of conception.

When people begin to behold the Subtle Plane, then they will be able to discern barely visible embryos that are already in the aura of those who will once give them life; but years may pass before a child comes into the world.

Think about the future of that seed of Fire, which you might be already carrying under your heart.

You need to demonstrate the consonance of harmony, so as not to be surprised at the eccentric character traits of your children.

I shall tell you one word, without making a mystery out of it: *Love...* is omnipotent.

And if you love, that means you are omnipotent.

PART I

If you want to achieve something in your life, do not resort to the powers that be, for they are weak.

But multiply the currents of Love, and I shall not know any human being stronger and more all-powerful than you on the Earth.

If you love, you will achieve everything.

I invest you with the Power of Love: take whatever you wish.

The world belongs to the heart which has come to love all humanity.

Offer heaven to everyone.

Let not even an earthly shadow flicker in your word, but may it slide in as a weightless little cloud, touching the dormant mind with its wing.

The Light will awaken sleepers.

And they will turn their eyes to the empyrean, carried away by your word, revealing the beauty of Heaven.

To yield yourself prisoner is easy, laying down your weapon at the feet of the enemy.

But do mercy and a righteous life then await you?! No!

Even they will despise you, for one who has betrayed once will always be capable of betraying.

Turn not into a Judas, for bitter is the lot of humanity's waste.

I am singing the Song of Heroic Deeds, but traitors will never understand it.

Take up the Song of Love, O My warrior!

They will spin new "yarn" of your destinies, and all threads will lead towards Me.

The patterns woven by bright Love will enchant the eyes of Distant Worlds.

I sanctify everything by My Name, enhancing silver threads by firmness and brightness.

The pattern of the stars is forever indestructible.

30 October

The Light will pour out from Above.

And gloomy walls will collapse, melting like wax in the warm flame.

The darkness cannot put obstacles for your spirit if you have a fiery aspiration.

The Fire is your pass to all the worlds.

It will allow you to enter all the spheres which have previously been inaccessible to you.

The junction of two Eras has been pointed out as the last period, and these will converge in the near future.

The old and the New cannot merge together, just as it is not proper to leave a corpse next to a living being;

they will not get along well under the same roof: the stench of decomposition can destroy all life.

Yet it is still necessary to allot a few moments to say goodbye.

So, bid kind farewell to the world which has outlived its time.

I shall rejoice at your successes as a parent rejoices at the first steps of a small child.

I am empowered to behold the stellar pace of your spirit.

And it delights Me already today.

It is a shame that nothing frightens man so much as his own stupidity.

The least drop of self-criticism makes it possible to cope with any vice.

However, people look for them in others rather than in themselves.

Foolish are they who draw attention to the faults of others before their own.

Give a smile to a passer-by, and do not feel sorry for the particle of Light you gave away, just as a tree does not grieve over the leaves falling from its crown.

Be wise and know that your smile will be born again and again, like an emerald leaf that appears on a tree in the place of a fallen one.

A smile is your cross.
Bear it with a smile.

There is a lot of work to be done on the Earth, and its boundlessness should only delight the spirit aspiring for ceaseless labour.

Rejoice when you touch an unwieldy load, then you will be able to lift a load even heavier than you could ever imagine.

One gives a smile, the other — an evil grin.

And both of them serve: one — the Light, the other — the darkness.

Whom do you serve, O man, rushing from one extreme to the other?

Are you not standing still, being torn by contradictions?

Choose your path and follow it; after all it is impossible to simultaneously ascend towards a mountain top and descend to the netherworld.

Know your path, O man!

31 October

They will forget about you, prophets, and your names will be erased from the pages of history.

But I shall give you new names, and again you will set out for a journey, continuing to build the structure you started.

PART I

And they will call the finished Temple in your name, and will begin to serve the One who sent you to achieve feats of arms.

You are serving in His Name, being concealed beneath garments of various names.

Heaven alone knows your secret name that will forever be indelible on the pages of Fiery History.

The servants of darkness, in trying to steal your treasure, undertake a series of attacks, but they only temper your armour by their continual strikes.

The armour of the spirit must be strong and impenetrable.

But at the same time I am telling you about your inner softness and pliability.

Repel a spear, but take to heart someone's call for help, which is barely perceptible to the ear.

May the Light of the treasure manifest therein multiply someone's forces, thereby helping them to repel the enemy's spear.

Save the treasures of the world — human hearts.

I shall be extremely disappointed if I behold you in deep despondency.

I who am tirelessly talking about Joy do not want to remind you of that so often, but still I have to.

And how can I remain silent when I see your face submerged in sorrow?

Why do you direct your gaze into gloom when you are serving the Light?

Distress not your heart, which aspires to the Fire.

And rejoice My Heart with the light of your smile.

Words dedicated to Love will flow out into the world like an avalanche.

A New Round requires new speeches.

Leave obsolete words to past days.

Do not try to take them into tomorrow, for thereby you will only weave a cobweb for yourself.

Liberate yourself from the shackles of yesterday and enter My New World unencumbered.

The warriors of Love will defend the conquests of Light with all their might.

They will feel their spirits rise at the sight of the commander, leading them into battle.

Does he need to hide as he sends forth his warriors?

No, he must be in the midst of the attack and, moreover, he must be the first to join the fight.

What is an army devoid of its leader worth?

I shall stand up with all My might, shielding My warriors who strive to attack in the name of the triumph of Love throughout the world.

PART I

Brothels will be closed, and the Fire will erase from the face of the Earth even the ashes of the human beings who built them.

Temples of Eternal Beauty will soar to the highest heights, enchanting human hearts by their sheer simplicity of creation.

Old buildings will seem absurd and ugly — moreover, they will be eliminated when it turns out there is no demand for them.

A house lives only as long as it is occupied, and it crumbles to dust when it is abandoned by all those who have lived there before.

I am building new houses for you — enter and live under My roof.

You will need to cope with thoughts that have slid across the pure vault of heaven like dark vultures.

A gloomy thought is constantly seeking out one which is born in the light, and it attempts to devour it by a single flap of its dark wing.

Do not let a little fledgeling be eaten by a vulture, but protect it fervently, firmly defending your frontiers.

Defeat evil with the Name of Maitreya, burning its dark feathers with the Flame of Love.

Raise light-bearing eagles, which are capable of perceiving the wisdom of mountains with their brave spirits.

1 November

Our Pilgrim has laid the foundation for future ages.

He came under different Names, and in the building process He employed many souls of those who were willing to share in the heroic labour.

And the long-time fellow-warriors are now erecting high walls.

The pattern, marvellously created in the depths of time, must reveal itself on the surface.

The crucifixion of Christ is not accidental, and the drops of sacrificial blood by no means fell in vain.

Sproutings have covered arable land which was formerly barren, and the Reaper is descending to the fields to gather the harvest of the seeds He sowed.

As for the army of militant fools, led by one of them, is it not doomed to perish before joining the fight?

But a sage at the helm will be able to lead the ship of fools to a harbour where they will find salvation and save others from the consequences of their own stupidity.

The time of wise people has come.

And it is foolish to deny their dominant role in a place one cannot pass through without a fiery thought.

Foolishness is the sign of the old world, while Wisdom is the mark of the Future Age.

PART I

It is essential to demarcate the boundaries of the mind.

Stand firmly on watch, and do not allow the spies of darkness to enter the Camp of Light.

Let them meet the most fervent rebuff so that they may experience the entire might of your fire, which scorches their shaggy paws.

Bright thoughts, like warriors, must always be on guard.

A fortress open wide to the enemy is in a dismal situation.

Bring forth the boundaries of Fire.

Galactic Wars are nothing new to humanity, for many science-fiction writers have described futuristic battle scenes.

But reality exceeds all human imagination.

And you have no idea of the dangers you are exposed to every moment.

Yet We must know this, since We have assumed the mission of protecting the whole human population of the Earth from terrible destruction.

The world stands at the brink of catastrophe, but We are singing confidently a hymn to tomorrow, knowing that it will be much more beautiful than the days that have gone before.

The Victory of Light is predetermined.

Climb the ascending rungs firmly: thousands of Galaxies await your steps, and your triumphant march already reaches their sensitive hearing.

We bring Victory to bright worlds.

Violent winds which attempt to tear My leafage from its mighty crown will stand still.

And the stronger the attacks, the tighter the leaf tries to cuddle up to My Tree.

Exposure to incessant attacks will only make it stronger.

Search not for peace amidst the storm, but find forces to withstand its gusts.

The time of winds is departing, and the peace of silence will most assuredly come.

It would be right to remember that the world is permeated with My Call.

Do not call those who have already been summoned and are now on their way, and, moreover, do not touch those who pretend not to hear My Call.

All are summoned.

Your task is to advance without pressuring or cursing stragglers along their way.

Hasten towards Me in such a way that will attract others by your example, drawing them into the fiery whirlwind of forward movement.

My Call is pervading the Earth.

PART I

The human burden is precious; otherwise, why would one carry it if it were worthless?

You must be born as Man in order to be able to become a God.

That is why the burden is priceless — because it is Divine.

Do not lose or spill it: it is a gift of the Immortal Fire.

I have come down to the Earth to help you become a God, O mortal man.

Come and join the assembly of immortal Gods!

2 November

A lot has been said of Joy, but I shall add one more adage: Joy gives wings.

Hence, Joy is that engine which is able to raise one up.

So do not shut it off, but maintain it in working condition, for sad is the fate of those who fall from a height they have achieved.

Why do birds soar smoothly and people alone fall down as stones?

Is it not because the bird's heart is nourished by the joy of flight, and is it not because man attempts to soar with a stone around his neck, increasing his weight with gloomy currents that bind him to the earth?

THE CALL OF THE HEART

Do not cut off your wings, O man; let them become stronger in flight by igniting a powerful engine of Joy within yourself.

Ancient adages are filled with exalted significance.

Like resplendent bridges, they have gained strength throughout space, because many have realized the value of their essence and ascended with their help.

The sustainability of those thoughts has been cemented over the course of centuries.

And if it is hard for you today, enter upon a resplendent bridge with the thought that "this, too, shall pass!"

The main thing is always simple: love the whole world!

How often does a person ask a natural question: What to do in life?

And My answer is simple: Love!

You can conquer this world only through Divine Love.

Rejoice in the successes of others, but not in your own, so as to temper your feeling of superiority.

Serve as a support point for those who want to push off in their quest to ascend even higher: their victory is your victory.

And the outpouring of the currents of your heart will not remain unnoticed by Me.

PART I

It is necessary to pay for joy, but an even greater payment is charged for sadness.

One must pay for each darkening with the fires of one's heart.

Is not this wastefulness madness, when I speak of the accumulation of treasures?

But at the same time I command you to be generous and give away your accumulated assets.

You should strive to comprehend what I have just said.

"Matter is primary, the spirit is secondary" — is not this what they teach you in earthly schools?

But I say that even more primary than either spirit or matter is the Celestial Fire.

It conceives both your spirit and matter, giving them life.

Know the primacy of substance, but do not abandon the priority of the spirit, which is predetermined on the earthly plane.

Eyes attempt to discern what lies beyond the border of the visible world.

It is not with the eye that we shall distinguish the subtle forms, but with the heart, which is capable of discerning everything hidden from the earthly eye.

The heart possesses the empyreal vision and already beholds how the New World will be different from the old world.

My World is coming, already marching with broad steps across the near-Earth expanses.

I am leading new builders along with Me, and I ordain them to build by Love alone.

3 November

The Ray of Love is pouring out ever wider, embracing incredibly vast expanses.

One cannot come out of water and be dry; thus the one who has dipped oneself into the flow of Divine Love is already marked by her currents.

There is no escape from the all-pervading Fire, and the Transfiguring Flame will be creating within every heart, composing the melody of Fiery Love.

Put together all of your treasures accumulated over thousands of lives, and marvel at their light.

But remember that, just like an experienced diver plunging into the abyss of earthly waters, you have gathered them not only for yourself.

Catch pure pearls in your cupped hands and bring them to the world, so as to offer to the poor in spirit a little grain of Fiery Truth.

And may the brightness of your treasures illuminate the way of those who walk in darkness.

PART I

Foresight is the gift of the coming Age.

It is vital to know the patterns of destiny in order to further their manifestation on the earthly plane in every possible way.

A septenary pattern is composed for each body, and none of them should break the pattern predestined for another.

All of them are interrelated, skilfully intertwined by the subtlest threads.

Synchronize the earthly pattern only by the Empyreal one, but not vice versa, as the lower should not rule over the higher.

The border of Light is subtle where darkness reigns.

One cannot say that it is absolute in the depth of its gloom.

A certain part of the substance of the spilled Light still exists; it penetrates the depths of darkness, according to Cosmic Laws.

A chance to ascend is provided to everyone, and bright rungs will immediately show up, if you have an overwhelming desire to get close to the Light, O you who thirst for the Fire after a long stay in pitch darkness.

Behold the boundary of Light — it is present everywhere.

The flesh and the spirit have different substances, yet still they must be connected by a single wire which establishes a harmonious relationship between them.

But the currents of Love alone will demonstrate the proper tension, manifesting a harmonious tuning between elements that are in evident contradiction to each other.

Without Love you are nothing, but with Her — you are Gods!

Sufferings will run dry — each leaf of My Tree is working at this, absorbing all the dust and dirt for further processing within its internal laboratory.

They are My children, who bring purification, burning by the fires of their compassionate hearts all the pain and grief existing in the world.

And their work is visible to Me.

And I can say that with every moment of heartfelt labour the world becomes purer and, as a result, the current of suffering decreases within the entire Human Race.

Labouring in the name of Divine Love is the most important thing in the world.

Nothing will move forward or climb a rung on the Ladder of Evolution if it is unable to perceive the currents of Love and to assimilate the stellar substance flowing out from all the celestial bodies.

PART I

Go with Love, if you wish to reach God, for His Name is... Love!

Bangalore
4 November

I am composing hymns to hearts.

I am composing a human Song, but not an angelic one: man on the Earth is ordained to be Man and to live a human life.

Disfigure not yourself, trying to make yourself out to be an angel.

Be, above all, a human being of full value, and Angels will rejoice when they behold you.

You will ascend not by ugliness, but by beauty, representing the perfection of Man within yourself.

Leave Angels to their spheres and do not attempt to replace them with yourself.

Everyone is assigned their place in the world to perfect themselves limitlessly within it.

The Ladder of Evolution itself will take you to new rungs, composing hymns to the triumph of simple human genius.

Old castles are crumbling and old plans are collapsing, built as they are on sand.

But the Leaders of Light are vigilantly standing guard, illuminating new patterns.

Construction projects are aspiring heavenwards and the Plan of Lords will be implemented no later than their predetermined periods.

Satya Yuga is firmly strengthening upon the foundation formed before.

The Earth is trembling and shaking from the blows of falling stones, but this pain is sacred: through it the recovery of the entire world, worn out as it is with suffering, will occur.

Yet it could be even worse if people, at the instigation of the darkness, continue to destroy themselves and the surrounding world.

Many, too many troubles and misfortunes have been brought about by the weak-mindedness of humanity!

However, a wise thought has still managed to make its way towards human hearts.

Thus, the thought of the heart has prepared salvation for the whole world.

And things can no longer get worse, for the Age of Heart is entering upon all the Earth's expanses.

Concentrate your thought on the heart — and you will perceive the currents of the Divine Wisdom.

Put into action the Word I have spoken, and you will immediately feel the full power of the currents assisting you in your intended plan.

PART I

My Word is the key which can open any door.

But if you do not make an effort, and do not turn the key in the hole, then the door will remain locked.

I gave you My Word to put into action.

Grace and Beauty are unchangeable earthly companions, going hand in hand with the supreme spirit.

And if people's acts are marked with their seal, you will be able to discern whether a spirit comes from the Light or from the darkness.

Those who are advancing towards the Heavenly Fire are brimming over with Divine Beauty.

My friends, My enemies are all dear to Me: sometimes friends contribute to a fall, and enemies — to an ascent.

We become stronger from blows, but not from flattering words.

An enemy can become a friend, while a friend is often capable of becoming an enemy.

Value everyone equally, for you never know how changeable earthly faces are.

Always undertake new ventures and never keep in mind the thought that something might be impossible.

Everything is possible when you advance in consonance with My currents.

The mighty stream of Sacred Love will lift you, carry you on wavecrests to goals which before seemed unattainable.

Go with Maitreya and attempt to align your steps with His.

I shall help you align your step with Mine.

Pondicherry
5 November

People have become utterly lost in the wilds of their searches.

And I pointed out the trail of salvation, but not everyone was willing to use it.

Many preferred to plunge ever more deeply into impassable thickets, getting their feet bogged down in marshy swamps.

After all, My Brothers have warned you that your shout cannot be heard from the bottom of the swamp, if you have a silent heart: it is only its voiceless cry that We can hear.

Know the language of the heart, O man!

Wisely ponder the errors resulting from your conclusions.

Persist not in your blunders, stubbornly insisting like a fool on your own opinion.

PART I

Find a grain of truth in a contrary opinion, then the kingdom of the negating mind will come to an end.

Reveal Truth within your heart.

Most importantly, avoid scorning any situation and accept calmly, and with equanimity, everything life sends your way.

If you are dissatisfied with little, you will evoke even greater dissatisfaction through your consonant currents; and, if you are satisfied with little, you will imperceptibly attract to yourself the currents of supreme bliss.

I am teaching you to cope with all circumstances in your life.

Give rest to your mind by stopping its chaotic and bustling run.

And in the resulting silence, look into the depths of your pure heart — and you will find there hundreds of thousands of beautiful thoughts that could not break through to you, obscured as they were by a clamouring flock of dark ravens.

Listen to the silence of your heart.

Even a single word will be sufficient to ignite the hearts of those who walk in gloom, but this word should become your essence and be reflected in each beat of your pulse — Love!

Inhale her currents with your flaming heart and exhale into the world at least a particle of My Fire, and you will obtain Eternity — the Eternity of Divine Love.

I shudder at the sight of those who have assumed the burden of earthly leadership, hiding under the name of "Light."

Coming from the gloomy darkness, they do not see what fate awaits them.

Their dark hearts, like small pieces of coal, will be charred by the hot Flame and turn into grey ash.

But they do not know what they are doing — this was said to them long ago.

Meet Maitreya, who is coming into the world, joyously, dissipating any doubt about His Advent.

Marvel at His Face of Light, for He bears within Himself a reflection of the Divine Flame, marking those who follow Him with the seal of Fire.

The seal of Love is blazing upon the brow of everyone advancing towards Me, shining as a bright star.

A fiery-white page of History has been ignited in human hearts.

Welcome Me.

PART I

Adyar
6 November

Blind forces are leading apostates into battle, dooming them in advance to perdition.

They need only inject their stings, and after that even the embrace of death is not frightening: at the cost of life, they are ready to inject poison!

But you must not blindly expose yourself to their venomous bites either, otherwise the gift of divine vision will never touch you.

It is hard for the blind to be led by the blind.

The servants of darkness are creeping, stealing up to awakening human hearts — they want both to steal the fire and to remain unnoticed in the theft of someone else's flame.

But their pockets will not be able to hold their ill-gotten gains, and their shaggy paws will be scorched by heat which they cannot tolerate, let alone withstand.

Do not bring retribution upon your heads, servants of deep gloom.

Do not stain your souls, for, after they are deprived of the reflection of light, the defeat they suffer will plunge them into the abyss of despair.

Why steal something that My children are ready to give you in any case?

Only reach out to them with your hearts — and, with all the flaming magnanimity of those hearts, you will be endowed with the Fire.

Aspire to rise higher in any situation.

And, even if you are on the verge of despair, humiliation, and violation, you can still maintain the high position predestined for you by the Empyreal World.

I hold high the flame of your heart, and you must not disparage My Fire, losing your brightness to the slightest feeble efforts of gloom.

Hold My Light as high as you possibly can.

One's main aspiration in life should be to reach the Fiery Heights.

That is why I say unto those who have chosen the Light of Evolution: look forward only, for the speed of the one who looks back is equal to naught.

The purpose of the path is clearly shining ahead.

Otherwise there is no point in leaving your home if you do not wish to achieve anything.

We can gauge our loyalty to the earthly world only by Empyreal measures.

Those who serve Me, honour both the earthly and the Heavenly in equal measure.

Hold the pans of the scales in a grand balance so that I can see your loyalty, which nothing can disturb.

Be vigilant during all your earthly days and nights and do not blunt your sharp gaze — either by the glitter of apparent gold and gems or by the sheen of someone else's glory.

Be ever blind to perishable treasures, yet be alert to the brilliance of pearls tightly tucked within their shells, covered by the sand of oblivion.

Alertness is inherent to My warriors, and they are to be always armed therewith, as long as gloom rages, attempting to undermine the values of the Empyreal World by substituting the mundane.

Know the price of things when I am speaking about the priceless quality of alertness.

Build your new day with bright colours.

Begin each morning in a new way, and just as you are capable of drawing a marvellous pattern on a sheet of white paper, so paint your day with currents of unprecedented beauty.

May the White Colour of Maitreya embellish each new day.

7 November

It is possible to demonstrate one's devotion to a Fiery Ray by a variety of means.

It is not necessary to create artificial forms of ritual worship, but it is more essential to lay on the altar at least one piece of fruit, nurtured by good deeds.

We cannot get used to hypocrisy, and We should not engage in it, especially when I have urged you to engage in relations dictated by Beauty.

You should build your life by collaborative measurement with it alone.

Give your thoughts a rest, and your weary legs as well, not rushing after the first idea you see that is but vaguely manifested.

Calm your mind and allow your heart to say a word.

Trust that its silence will bring you thousands of the most beautiful thoughts — thoughts that will never be feasible for the mind.

The product of the human mind is not always suitable for food.

And no matter how spiritually hungry you are, do not seize the first books you see and swallow them indiscriminately — you might poison yourself that way.

Be discriminating when taking spiritual food.

You can say everything, but you must remember that you will have to bear responsibility for all the thoughts you express; and it is good when they are beautiful; otherwise you have only yourself to blame.

I shall protect all of you who walk through life in My Ray.

And may nothing confuse your mind at the hour when pitch darkness thickens around you.

You will head towards victory together with Me, after multiplying the Flame of Fiery Glory.

I shall tell you about Love, but you need to listen sensitively, for amidst the noisy bustle of life it is hard to hear the Voice of My Heart.

Immerse your heart in silence — and you will hear the beatings of My Heart, which sings for you about Divine Love.

8 November

All the human hearts capable of nurturing the luminous thread linking them with the Distant Worlds are occupied with the assimilation of the currents now approaching the Earth.

Help comes to the planet every moment, and, like an experienced surgeon's scalpel, rays cut out any malignant excrescence.

A mortally sick body requires revitalization and diligent care so that the recovery proceeds with all possible speed.

Work hard.

Blessed is the labour of your heart.

Uncompromising decisions requiring a rigid approach must often be made in respect to some action or another.

Do not make one-sided judgements based on the single facet you are able to see.

Remember that multifacetedness can be based on binarity.

Do not renounce it without seeing the entire pattern of your future, hidden from your eyes for the time being, fogged by a shroud of tears.

I have said: Remember the multifacetedness of all Creation!

You can distinguish the boundaries of Light and darkness; you need only to strain the eye of the heart and it will suggest to you the true colours of everything manifest in the surrounding world.

Do not step blindly when you have the All-Seeing Eye.

Tea plantations are spread all across India, but many are seduced by the smell of tobacco.

And the space allotted for a particular kind of plant is often targeted by others.

The struggle takes place not only in the Human Kingdom, but also in the Kingdom of Vegetables, not to mention the Animal Kingdom.

PART I

How to explain to human beings that some plants have emanations which are vitally necessary for the breathing of the planetary body?!

They are ready to stop the outflow of vivifying currents for the sake of their own pleasure and to permeate everything with fetid smoke, conveying nothing but death and preparing for suffocation from the poisons they produce.

Take a closer look at each leaf you are attempting to grow and see whether it will bring life or death to the altar of service to humanity.

Bask in the Sun when he shines brightly, and conceal yourself from rain just as that celestial body hides behind the clouds.

Does the Sun lose his warmth when the clouds disperse?!

No, he shines with the same warmth he had before!

So must you, clouded by grief, anguish, and resentment, conceal your face from the trenchant blows of hail and be higher than the hostile source which showers them upon you.

A cloud will empty itself, as it is unable to withstand its own heaviness.

But you radiate as before, brightly and clearly.

Let nothing touch you in this world.

The Path of the Sun was predetermined for you long ago.

The clouds are gathering, and an avalanche of rain is about to pour out into the world.

Why do they crowd so tightly and blindly rush at each other, summoning the peals of thunder produced by their mighty strokes?

Is it not the light that the strike was to ignite?

So, during the collisions of life, know that the stronger the blow that has been struck, the brighter will be the fiery flash that must illumine you.

People, like dark thunderstorm clouds, are gathering around you, trying to firmly cover the entire space with cement.

But you should welcome every cloud appearing on your horizon: it comes to increase and enhance the Light of your heart.

It is easy to isolate yourself and fence yourself off from hostile influences, but why then did you descend into this world, taking on a heavy cross in the process?

To share human sufferings!

How can you alleviate another's lot when you turn away from them, and blindly shut yourself away behind an iron door?

I did not send you to hide in the caves but to be in the midst of suffering people and to generously give out My ethereal treasures, multiplied by the Light of your loving heart.

PART I

Do you hide from those you love?

On the contrary: you desire to be with them every moment!

And if you wish to be with Me, you need to be in the very thicket of My beloved humanity — and thus you will be closer to Me.

I have spoken.

M.

PART II

Russia

Vladivostok
29 November

I am dropping the leaves of My Garden on coastal sand, and the breaking waves wash away their traces.

Time buries everything like a seasoned gravedigger, sweeping away all the dust from the face of the Earth.

But I shall not get tired from strewing the emerald leaves on the path of those who came into the world with My Name, who foresee the entire Divine Pattern by their spirit.

Time has no power to remove the trace left in the souls sanctified by the touch of the leaves of My Garden.

I am awakening a whirlwind of new currents coming into the world, originating from the bowels of the Sacred Himalayas.

One who enters the New Round will succeed in rising to the unprecedentedly high rung of Evolution.

Go together with the new people who descended into the world to help you to rise higher.

Do not look back on those who live in the past.

My birds must fly, in spite of the snares set for them.

Do not let them throw a bridle on your wings.

Regardless of time, construct your plans, confidently projecting your thought into the future.

As a mountaineer climbs towards the top, so you, too, should aspire towards your goal, and you will conquer all the Empyreal Peaks.

Always remember the main thing: the reason you came down to the Earth.

Neither to drink nor to eat, but to multiply spiritual nourishment.

And as you nourish your body, do not forget that your spirit will remain hungry, if you do not take care of it.

And it is possible to satiate the spirit only within earthly spheres, where it must gather up the deposits of imperishable treasures.

PART II

The body exists for the sake of your spirit, but not the other way round!

So, remember.

If you bow to everyone you meet, will not you get a humpback by loading yourself down with other people's opinions?

Thoughts of doubt and rejection will pile up as gravestones.

Stand aside, for a rockfall threatens to come down upon you, if you have fallen under the influence of hostile forces.

Straighten your back and look proudly into the eyes of Truth, paying no attention to the hail of stones flying after you.

And do not throw it under foot in order to please the opinion of the first person you meet.

But bow to the bearer of the Light of My World and know that you will stand up much straighter on account of this pure obeisance your heart has made.

Bow your head before the Great Spirit!

Earthly bells have fallen silent, and Nature has become still in anticipation of the Great Advent.

And only My warriors can know the time of the Supreme Descent, for the Fire of Heaven has engraved those periods in their hearts.

I am waiting for the last strike of the bell, heralding the news that the world of the Earth is ready to receive Me, but it must also resound within your heart.

After finishing their discourse on Truth, the prophets left, and the world once again covered their works with cobwebs and mould, making them quite unsuitable as food for hungry souls.

However, the light of knowledge has not grown dim, and the seed, not knowing decay, is reviving like a sphinx.

Love will pass through all the arable lands on the Earth, and the ripe grain, reared by the divine currents, will begin to come into its own.

The world, not knowing hatred and enmity, will kneel before the omnipotence of Sacred Love, and the Beauty of Her Light will reign supreme over the world eternally.

30 November

Regardless of the constructions of the darkness, the New World is erecting Temples.

Neither on sand nor on stone are We building walls, but within your hearts full of prayer.

They will stand impervious, for We are strengthening Our structures by the mixture of Fire.

PART II

You will marvel at your Temple, and worlds will bow before its beauty.

The mundane things are dominant in the world, instead of the *supermundane* — this is why all misfortunes happen.

But why should you wonder at failures, if perishable things are given top priority in your minds?

Get rid of yesterday's rubbish and do not bind your wings with outdated dogmas.

Gauge your steps not by earthly but by Empyreal measures — that way you will not even notice when success comes and changes your whole life.

The summands of success will be duly calculated if you know what result you wish to see.

And if you want to obtain a desired chemical reaction, you will not add something that is not included in the formula.

In the same way, if you desire to find mutual love, you need to eliminate thoughts of hatred and put together only those summands that bear the Light of Love within themselves — the feedback you get will surpass all your expectations.

Everyone wants to taste happiness, but this fruit is rarely accessible.

And it does not matter if someone passes away without ever having tasted what they desire: their quest will continue in the Ethereal Worlds.

And the soul will find peace in the gardens they will find scattered through stellar Infinity.

The fruit of Divine Happiness is awaiting everyone, and whoever reaches My Garden will certainly taste it.

Cold leaves its imprint on human relationships, but warmth melts ice.

That is why I ask My warriors not to extinguish their heartfelt warmth, for the slightest cool breeze towards their fellows may cost them their lives.

The servants of darkness may blow cold, while for you cooling down is equal to a crime.

Go forth like a fiery torch, thawing hearts which have been frozen from the cold of human indifference.

Save the world with your warmth!

All are equal before God: flower, snail, and man, but each has their own distinct worth.

Yet you should not attempt to evaluate anyone, for your scale of values cannot be compared with the one accepted in the Heavens.

You may easily make a mistake, tipping the scales in your favour.

Do not be so self-confident as you pluck the flowers of the Earth: life may demand an exorbitantly high payment from you, which you may end up paying off over more than one century.

Treat all creations of God with tender care, knowing that He has endowed not a single one of them with breath in vain.

Be confident in one thing: Life knows the price of everything — including your judgements, and your assessments, too.

Do not try to outwit life, for through your cunning you might end up weaving your own snares.

Becoming the treasure of the world is not a difficult task, but you will succeed only when you value a roadside stone or a dust-covered flower higher than yourself.

The planet is veering off the beaten track and rising to a new cycle.

Have there not been enough signs poured out for you already to indicate the global changes taking place in the world?

Do not search for evidence in formulas and secret calculations; they are all scattered in plain sight.

And the changing climate is the first evidence of this.

Spring is coming!

Sacred Spring is preparing to unfold all the flowers of My Garden and shoot forth all its emerald leaves.

The unprecedentedly marvellous time has come: the blossoming is gaining momentum!

The coming of My Spring will transform the whole world.

Get ready for the New, for I am bringing it every moment.

1 December

Let us continue to gather the leaves which have been so richly shed by the trees of My Garden.

You perhaps do not yet realize how happy and wealthy I wish to make you.

With each leaf you put to another, you form a rung, thereby granting a chance to ascend to those who strive to collect imperishable treasures.

This will give both yourself and others a chance to rise to the ultimate height by gathering the leaves of My Garden.

It is necessary to think over everything and to lay a firm thought upon the heart, whereby it may serve as a touchstone for your thinking and test its steadiness.

A small thought, weak and dark as it is, will not withstand the life-giving currents and will show forth its deathly nature; while a bright thought, on the other hand, will shine even brighter and reveal the whole beauty of the imperishable Fire.

Think through the Light!

PART II

Crying and grieving — that is the lot of weak souls.

And only those who, from the bottom of the abyss, are ready to strike the spark of a heroic deed, are strong in spirit.

"Crying will not help" — this is something you have known for a long time, yet you still cry and shed bitter tears.

No, My children, I do not come to you in order to wipe away your tears; in fact, I wish to dry them by the Heavenly Fire so that never again will I see you crushed by earthly grief.

I am bringing you the Light of Joy and permeating your hearts with it.

I am leading all the worlds towards Unity, weaving the patterns of destiny in a new way.

There are no tears in My plans — Joy alone radiates therefrom!

The main thing is not to despair in any situation and, while maintaining your balance, call upon all the Forces of Light so that you may find a way of salvation.

A right solution will definitely appear.

But they who despair interrupt the currents for themselves, thereby blocking access to a marvellous thought sent down from Heaven.

Believe in yourself, and you will win in any situation.

I place a book at the crossroads.

The Book of Destinies of all the peoples of the world will be accessible to you.

And, after leafing through all the pages, you will find yourself in it, and your heart will learn why you came to this people.

Do not hurry to curse your destiny and do not stigmatize your compatriots — your brethren.

It does not befit you to act like a blind person, when I present the Light of Insight to everyone.

I wish to see you as a creator of people's destinies and inscribe your name in the pages of Fiery History by My own Hand.

Upon taking a look at the world openly, you may be terrified, but imbue it with the rapture of your spirit, ready to bring in the Light of Transfiguration.

The Book of Feats is opened and awaiting you.

Discord and misunderstanding is all around — so why must you remain within that circle?!

Would not it be better to break through beyond the designated borderline, and soar upward in free flight?

Do not allow the ring to close around you; bravely make your way forward, for the trap might snap shut when you least expect it.

Be flexible: Life is found in movement, while death lies in wait in mortal immobility.

Fly up safely, and I shall support your flight.

Break the cycle of hopelessness and enter a New Round, which bears the Joy of Liberation.

The splash of waves of intercosmic currents comes with unprecedented might.

All the worlds are on trial, and every living creature is tested for its suitability for Life.

It is impossible to hold back the onslaught of energies pouring out as a powerful waterfall.

And one cannot block the way for the Messengers of the Empyreal World, advancing throughout the world with My Message.

Maitreya is coming!

The silent tread of His White Steed is resounding like a booming and awakening echo.

The Era of Love is neither fairy tale nor fiction, but the breath of the coming day.

It is not worth going against the flow of Fire, but one should think about how to enter the New Round, so as not to be engulfed in the vortex of elements, sweeping away all the rotten leaves into the hot Flame.

Step confidently into the Future — it is beautiful!

2 December

The sweetness of dreams affords an opportunity to touch spheres woven by invisible currents.

How limited man is in his vision and how pathetic is he in his reasoning, fettering himself in an iron vice!

There is an invisible world — yes, there is — no matter how often you deny this.

Does the Sun exist for the blind, and can they describe the entire charm of a blossoming flower, when all their evidence is concealed by darkness?

But the celestial body never ceases to exist, despite the fact that people do not admit the existence of the Fire.

So worlds stand firmly, with enviable generosity sending down currents to those who greedily devour them, at the same time stuffing their brains with coarse negation.

So why do you want to become like the blind — not only that, but are ready to follow someone who is blindly leading you to perdition?

Are there so few sighted people around?

The heart alone is capable of selecting a guide through life, for it possesses the capacity for fiery discernment.

Entrust yourself to the Fire: it will lead you along the shortest path and will pierce like lightning the invisible veil that previously hid from you all the infinite Beauty of Creation, full of countless worlds, invisible to the earthly eye but accessible to the heart.

PART II

A dream provides wings, it guides and endows us with unprecedented insight.

The sweetness of dreams will spread wide the wings of the fiery heart.

Fly to My World!

I shall repulse your enemy, covering you with My Fiery Shield.

Do not look back on those who slander you with their snake stings, vomiting malodorous venom upon the gawkers surrounding them.

What can be more hateful for ordinary people than the seeking heart, rebelling against the deadness of stagnation!

And no one could cause even greater hatred than the bearers of Divine Love: the wicked are ready to crucify everyone and to shower stones upon the pure heart, open wide towards their ferocious malice.

They would have torn you to pieces long ago if it were not for My Shield reliably protecting you from their poisonous arrows.

Bring Love, and cast away all the thoughts of doubt: Victory will always be ours.

Calumnies and conjectures always accompany Our Pilgrim.

Do not fear your ignorant and spiteful critics, but love them purely and sincerely.

The currents of Love will transform all of your persecutors, being carried away by their pursuit of the trail of Flame.

And Saul, running with a stone in his bosom, will become an Apostle.

The past cannot be returned, therefore there is no point in grieving for it.

It is human nature to embellish the past, yet let us not gaze at luxuriant flowers on graves, but rather let us set up a beautiful garden and grow a fragrant flowerbed on brand new soil.

Look forward: there are gifts ready and waiting for you; you just need to approach them with human footsteps.

Give to beggars, but not a scruffy piece of paper that will only discourage them from working and receiving payment for their sweat.

If we mindlessly begin to throw money into every outstretched palm, we shall grow a generation of soulless drones.

Hands must be used for labour.

Help the soul gone astray by your spirit and share the Fire generously, so that you may give impetus to the unresponsive heart and awaken it to life.

Give of whatever riches you have, and remember that mad people will remain mad, no matter what you offer them.

PART II

First look into their eyes and make sure that they are really ready to accept what you can give them.

Have you not had enough of casting pearls before swine?

You are coming to stop spiritual poverty, and once it is eradicated, everything else will come about in due course.

Except for the Sacred Fire, I can give you nothing: I come from the Flaming Spheres, bringing you that which My World has in abundance.

Neither silks nor gold do I wish to share with you, but with the priceless treasures that can enrich only the heart.

If you multiply the Light by My Gifts, you will never know poverty.

All worlds will belong to you.

I lay the Universe at your feet, go confidently into your boundless domains — the Fire is always ready to obey and serve the loving heart.

Love entitles you to possess everything — it is important to know this.

As you gaze at the starry sky, find accommodation for the Beauty of Creation in your heart.

Peer through the eyes of your heart into bottomless depths, concealing myriads of emerging new orbs.

At the appropriate time, they will unfold their own worlds; these may not resemble the life of the Solar

System, but they will not contain evil or violence, once these spores are destroyed and the seed of darkness is unable to reproduce itself.

Be mindful of the destinies of thousands of galaxies, and ponder the responsibility before Creation for every thought and deed you generate.

Create worlds by Love!

3 December

A special path is prepared for those who walk in the name of the Lord.

There is no gnashing of teeth or tears of despair — their path is strewn with Joy.

And if scary howlings begin to arise within, you know that you have deviated from the flaming path.

The sacred procession of Joy started long ago, yet of those summoned only a few have joined.

Know your ordained path and do not be enticed by someone else's pathway, for its smoothness is deceptive and a trap may be densely concealed under false flowers — so that you might be decoyed by the splash of their colours.

Do not yield to the illusion of the path, but, once you stand firmly on your pathway, do not hesitate to walk confidently, harbouring in your breast the Name of the Lord; this will serve as a guiding star for you.

PART II

They may indeed scoff at you, but do not lose your sense of balance.

Further, be sure to maintain a feeling of heartfelt warmth towards your persecutors: they serve Me as though raging dogs were rushing after you to drive you towards My Fiery House.

It was said long ago: "Everything will turn out for the Good."

Yet their incessant barking will awake many slumberers, and their sharp fangs will remind you to be alert.

All serve the good of Evolution, you only need to notice this, and not hide behind lying speculations, which are convenient for a mind filled with negation.

And while deniers suffocate from their own fury, you will carry the light of smiles to My altar, remembering that "this too shall pass!"

The caravan goes on despite the dogs' barking, and the graceful movement of the "ships of the desert" leaves no doubt that the quicksand will be left behind, and the goal will be achieved in time, cargo preserved.

Neither will the cameleer fear the venomous scorpions which teem in abundance amid the hot desert, nor the burning Sun nor the winds which skilfully bury all living things under dunes — all these will only hasten the caravan and dictate the urgency of the chosen path.

We welcome independent aspirants.

Only those who have reached Us by their own steps are valuable to Us.

And let them not delude themselves: those who come flying like vultures to My unfledged little bird, attempting to peck it to death, will never pass into My Kingdom.

They are trying to tear to shreds the heart which has brought you My Gifts.

However, it is no more possible to crucify the rays of the Sun than the fiery orb himself.

Think, at least attempt, if you have not lost sobriety of mind: why do I need blind people?

It is not drones that I wish to breed amidst stellar gardens, but High Creators, prepared to carry out never-ending labour.

It is possible to ascend the Ladder of Evolution only by your own steps, not someone else's — such is the Law of Heaven.

And anything that is not able to stand fast will be swept away by a single whirlwind of Fire.

A little piece of ice is floating, exuding its cold into the surrounding water, but it is not aware of its impending doom, already losing its former shape with catastrophic speed, and soon it will dissolve and merge with an all-encompassing warm current.

PART II

Thus man, too, is still exuding ferocious malice, unaware that his planet has already been encircled by the currents of Fiery Love, which are burning up any wild impurities.

Spring has arrived on the Earth, and a thaw has appeared in the world.

A different Sun rises, one renewed in the Fires of the Great Heart of Maitreya, which are burning brighter than ever before.

The world will be saved, and all the ice-floes will most assuredly melt in the warmth of Love which has come down to you.

My children cry only with joy; they do not defile their eyes with self-pitying tears.

You descended into this world not for your own sake, but for the sake of rescuing those who are in need of heartfelt warmth.

Wipe all tears from the faces of those who have fallen to their knees and ignite the light of Joy within them.

Revelations are important, but it is not possible to impart them to everyone.

Those who distort the whole Light of Truth revealed to them will defile and condemn.

But We cannot abandon the world, allowing it to get bogged down in lies and gloomy illusions of life.

The Fire is coming!

Appearing around Our One Teaching pouring forth throughout all ages, this Fire is scorching a whole cobweb of human stratagems.

And I shall tell you frankly: in bringing Love, I am touching the heart of everyone with Her currents.

And I conclude My Teaching with one word: Love!

The One Religion is... Love.

Love will be established on your Earth.

4 December

A New Word is pouring forth across the vast expanses of the Earth.

We shall regard the essence of all manifest creation in a new way.

Nothing threatens one clothed in the currents of immortality, but one covered in the rags of decay must leave the stage of Life.

It is impossible to pass into My New World carrying outmoded yardsticks.

I mete out all things by a new measure and I offer it to you for your use: the more you apply the yardstick of Love to everything, the more quickly you will begin to live according to the new currents.

The Word of Love must be not on the lips but within the heart, so co-measure your life with it.

PART II

People will forget you and your descendants will not remember you unless you yourself see to it.

And if no trace is ever left, who will bother to follow your pathway?

Someone leaves bright milestones behind them, which serve as guideposts for searching hearts, while others leave behind only bloodstained footsteps.

Such traces are indelible — there is not enough time to discern the true colours of everything left to us as a heritage.

But you do have free will, and you are at liberty to choose your own way.

And to whom you aspire — and whether you will leave your own trace — depends upon you alone.

However, do not forget about the responsibility you bear to the entire Universe for your choice.

My Advent is preceded by two different phenomena: the gigantic cataclysms you yourself may behold, and the invisible things, inaccessible to the earthly eye.

You can track only what happens within the sphere of vision of your material body.

And if you already know that it has not a single but a sevenfold structure, you should understand how important the effects may be which are manifest beyond the borderline of the visible.

Do not thoughts govern all your actions and do not emotions give impetus to your astral body, endowing it with unbridled outbursts of anger?

Barriers had been placed for Me long before My coming near to human flesh, and this is why My descent began from those Spheres where your fiery spirit soars.

And if your heart receives Me, so your eyes will light up with the sparks of joy, you will reach out your hands towards Me, and direct your earthly steps towards Me.

Do not search Me with blind eyes, but look closely through the eye of your heart: the world is full of signs bearing witness to My Advent.

Your friends may do you a disservice with their excessive eagerness to help.

But do not condemn them for striving to be near and intervene in all the affairs of your life, attempting to give worthless instruction and advice.

They wish to serve to whatever extent they can, knowing no measure.

Do not judge them, but take action to protect yourself, so as to prevent intrusive visitors from turning into pesky flies.

They do not understand that help for a High Spirit must be provided in spirit; and a silent prayer of the heart will reach the goal faster than their idle talk about mundane affairs.

PART II

Those who steal your priceless time were mentioned long ago, but I shall add one more thing: My children should not indulge in any kind of theft.

Guard yourself fervently, and you will save the souls of many who might stray onto the slippery path of betrayal.

Do not allow them to poke into your private life, thus providing food for condemnation.

Keep yourself a secret and at the same time show the openness of your heart.

The path is hard, but when communicating with others you need to find a "golden mean."

Do not make enemies out of friends, but make the effort to demonstrate the opposite, so that a foe becomes your most loyal ally — this is your path.

The reward for labour is high.

One who has done work in spirit will be rewarded in spirit.

And do not set an earthly price or calculate an expected amount of payment for your Empyreal Work in advance.

Destiny itself will pay you, but in the coin you deserve.

Then you do not need to fear for the future, because now nothing will be taken away but, rather, something will be added.

A payment is set for everything in the world: work hard, and you will be rewarded a thousandfold.

Our warriors stand firmly on their feet, and the stronger the blows they experience, the more diligently they strive to maintain a balance.

It is unseemly to sway with the slightest breath of wind or rush in panic from piercing human glares.

I have armed you properly, protecting you by the Shield of Love, so use your weapon and fiery sword to cut off the dark hydra's venomous sting lurking behind your neighbour.

Save a little soul and give it a chance to ascend, resisting any gloomy delusions.

May it stand firmly on its feet, and I shall not fail to protect the newly minted warriors with My Shield of Love, for they have found shelter for their spirit in the Camp of Light.

The Lords have many Plans, but all of them are joined in the One Unified Plan, covering the long-suffering Earth with the most wonderful pattern.

The Sevenfold Flame is blossoming for the first time on your soil.

Make the effort to accommodate at least a particle of the Empyreal Light revealed to hearts and marvel at the feathering of the rays of the orbs now approaching you.

A New Era is coming, and nothing on the Earth is able to delay the advance of the invisible Fire.

Reconstruction will involve all the worlds and spheres of life.

Kali Yuga has come to an end, and Satya Yuga is already beginning to march across the earthly expanses, stepping out from the depths of the Flame of the Empyreal World.

Each particle of Fire reflects the Supreme Plan of the Lords, just as a drop contains all the properties of water.

The Fire and the Water will purify and cleanse the whole world.

Meet the dawn of the Era of Divine Love.

5 December

Your dream is being carried heavenward in search of those paths that will lead to the desired goal.

Of course, it is hard to find in the earth a force that is capable of fulfilling the high desire and embodying it into a concrete form — however, Heaven possesses the necessary might.

And if your thought reaches those Spheres which have such a miraculous ability, you can know that your dream will be clearly manifest in your earthly life.

So remember this: earthly patterns are woven in the Empyreal World.

The Flame of Love will soar high, fanning the entire planet by its warm breath.

Whether you want to acknowledge it or not, regardless of its acceptance or rejection, the Fire will knock on your doors as well, bursting in like an indomitable whirlwind.

You will not be able to block the way of the Omnipotent Flame, and should not even try, if you do not want to be swept away from the face of the Earth.

Openly welcome the new currents, for they have already reached your threshold.

Love the New in a new way.

My star is never sad: evenly and clearly it is shining at any given moment.

And this is how I wish to see you as well: as the scattering of fiery hearts which have ascended as celestial orbs.

Fires are extinguished from gloomy feelings, but the flame is magnified through bright Joy.

Make your choice on the above basis: do you want to grow Light or darkness within yourself?

And, once you have chosen the path of a star, do not extinguish your fire.

The planet is ascending in swift flight, invisible to the earthly eye, but We behold her movement and observe all the new currents that are already flowing in, setting the rhythm for the Earth's revolution in her orbit.

New seas and oceans are already forming, prepared to flood their destined soils in due time.

And new lands will reveal their bountiful fields, for the renewed Man is ordained to live in a new way.

Be not afraid of the coming changes, for I have come not to frighten you, but to invite you into My New World that will spread as a blossoming Garden throughout your planet.

It is a crime to grieve and flood the world with heart-breaking currents.

The bearers of My Light cannot surrender to despair and simply lower their hands, when emergency aid is required for all around who are in mourning.

Someone who has gotten into trouble does not need tears, but a friendly hand.

It is absurd for someone to sit on the edge of a deep pit and lament the fate of their neighbour who has fallen into it.

And if you happen to be by a swamp where someone is perishing, forget about your uplifting speeches and quickly concentrate all your efforts on rescuing the sufferer.

It is stupid to sing funeral dirges for your neighbours when there is still a spark of life glimmering within them.

Fan the flame, reviving the light of hope and offering the Joy of Salvation.

Reduce the number of those who tear Heaven apart with their screams of despair, and multiply the number of those who bring the light of smiles.

And, by your own example, illuminate the hearts ready to take up your Song of Joy.

It was excruciatingly painful, of course, but not once have you managed to turn back the onslaught of the forces of darkness.

And, if you have been victorious an endless number of times, you need not doubt that this time you will gain the upper hand once more and that the attacking host will retreat from you.

It is hard — and sometimes impossible — to live with a feeling of defeat, and so I ask you to avoid it, so that even through ages eternal you never again experience pain and suffering.

The invisible currents are advancing like a wall of Fire, new thoughts are rolling in like waves, and old buildings are collapsing with a bang.

The Armada of Rays is advancing, and the glow of fires is already enveloping many earthly spheres.

The Fire does not like compromises: it has exhausted all arguments and now is no longer willing to listen to false assurances.

One may envy its longsuffering patience, but there are periods when its patience is tested as well.

It does not tolerate lies, hypocrisy, or falsehood, which mask human barbarity.

The Fire's impatience only quickens its pace, and the tongues of the Flame rise up threateningly, ready to incinerate all that is so unbearably painful for it to behold in human form.

You cannot escape its fervent embraces and you cannot avoid the blazing Fire, which has risen up as a solid wall.

There is only one way out — namely, to become its colleague and flaming ally, bravely stepping forth towards the currents of the Holy Fire of Love.

6 December

The flaming heart serves as a magnet for spheres: everything is drawn to its life-bearing focus, which possesses an unparalleled power of attraction.

And new currents will pour in to nourish the fiery heart, and it will be afforded unprecedented opportunities.

Indeed, it will draw closer to the Creator, if it succeeds in creating new forms, immortalizing the structure in the rays emanating from Divine Love.

All of Our thoughts are directed towards the human heart, and the entire Universe awaits its transfiguration.

That is why My Teaching is addressed to hearts alone.

May the Light of Love be resurrected within them, and may the high Flame rise up to illuminate the whole world!

The heart is a great magnet, capable of attracting to itself all the Fire-breathing Spheres.

So do not reject the chance destiny has offered you; realize that you can become the Creator of your own universe.

My only concern is to envelop you more warmly with the currents of My Universal Love.

It is cold and lonely for you in the world, surrounded as it is by vicious currents of darkness.

I wish to cure many sores and cut off the malignant excrescences which have been engendered by your own efforts.

Love heals everything.

And if you want to be healed — you must love!

Scare away any thought sent to frighten you, and do not let it caw at the top of its lungs like a crow, muffling the chirping of God's birds.

PART II

Many thoughts attempt to nest within you, but you cannot admit them, for they will incubate others like them and start to whirl like a dark flock, predicting doom for both you and your neighbours.

Preserve the purity of your thoughts!

The number of songbirds across the Earth is far from negligible.

They are singing My Song, composing a melody in the Name of Maitreya.

Take a look around and see how many of those little birds have already become fully fledged, carrying My Message through all the domains of life.

They will reveal discoveries, they will affirm beauty, and they will immortalize new thoughts.

Hearken to their pure voices, and you will come closer to Truth.

I shall give you the New, but you should not come with an old jug, for then all the good moisture would leak out through its holes and cracks.

Place your open heart under the spout; I shall pour in My loving currents right to the very brim.

It is sinful to doubt, since at the root of doubt lies a seed of betrayal.

Go forward with confident affirmation, My warrior, and leave the path of negation to the servants of darkness.

And do not call the Light *darkness*, nor the gloom *fire*.

This mistake may cost you your life, and your own ignorance might throw you off the pathway of Evolution.

Relegate doubt to the darkness, for that is where it belongs, and remember that no Teaching of Light has ever commanded one to doubt.

Not only that, but the Teaching considers doubt a sin.

Do not sin against the Light, if you are following in its pathway.

Nazareth is glorious!

And Kurukshetra is glorious as well, and they will be renowned for dozens of decades, as they have both given life to Light-bearing Heroes.

The area for the birth of any Spirit is not chosen accidentally.

Here everything is planned and taken into account beforehand: where they are to be born, where they are to demonstrate their fiery valour, where they are to experience the glow of enlightenment, and where they are to reflect the Empyreal Works and receive the entire flow of descending rays.

Your geographical map is very different from the one possessed by the Lord of the Worlds.

We do not conform with earthly but with Empyreal scales when We are reshaping the world.

You will become witnesses to many changes, and the delight of Beauty will permeate your flaming heart.

The renewed Earth will be truly glorious, and its eternal Glory will resound even in the Distant Worlds.

7 December

You may encounter many obstacles on the way to the Light.

You cannot avoid or pass around them, for you cannot stray off into the gloom surrounding you on both sides.

You need to decide everything immediately, while the barriers have not yet grown to completely block your way.

But remember one thing: you yourself erect these obstacles by thoughts formed from your own doubts and fears.

Do not block the path for yourself!

We ascend not by our hopes, but by the actions we carry out with our human hands and feet.

It is not difficult to become a dreamer, but I call upon you to be a Creator, and discard all your earthly fantasies.

Think wider, embrace the entire boundless expanse of endless worlds, and you will succeed in rising from the dust; you will move with gigantic steps from star to star, immortalizing the fruits of creative thought.

Create the Light through the light of an exalted dream.

People will think that you are not of this world — and they will judge correctly.

And how could it be otherwise, if nothing temporal allures you by false colours and thereby attracts your gaze?

An eternal dissatisfaction with earthly treasures characterizes your stellar spirit, which seeks imperishable gifts and aspires with all its essence to reach invisible spheres.

It knows its Fiery Homeland, and nothing can tempt it in this world.

And so it dictates its terms, endeavouring to transform the whole human essence in the Divine Flame, and if it succeeds in achieving even the slightest part of the transmutation, this entitles people to believe you are "not of this world."

Where there is Light, there Deity abides; and where there is darkness, there is no point in looking for Divinity.

PART II

It is hard for the heart to reach out to someone gloomy and spiteful, when their very appearance is repulsive.

And how bright it can be in the soul after communication with those who have abated your pain by their cordiality and geniality.

Learn to discern those who pass through life with the seal of Light and the label of darkness, so as not to mistake the servants of gloom for a Deity.

By contrast, you can determine the servants of Light by the light they exude.

If you try and claim that you were such and such a person in your past life — the common people will only laugh at you.

Many are still not ready to cross the borders of ignorance.

But thus they will ridicule their own ignorance, not you — you who have penetrated the mystery of your own history.

And if you see the people unprepared to perceive your word, so do not attempt to argue with them further, for that will provoke even more mockery.

Why would they need to know who you were?

You are the one who must know this!

The Human Tribe lives a hard life because those who attempt to cultivate a herd mentality have only recently been released themselves from their animal skins.

Their leaders are trying to bring you to a dead end, constantly competing among themselves to be a trendsetter.

They can only take you backwards, inculcating their bestial instincts.

But I am calling you to *freedom*, leading you by your *free will*, endeavouring to liberate from human skin the stellar spirit that will carry you away to the invisible expanses of the Universe.

I want to make you Creators — the Gods of new worlds.

There is no way back for man, when a high rung on the Ladder of Evolution is shining ahead.

You are Gods!

Always remember this.

In overcoming the chain of obstacles in its path, the spirit aspires to soar to Flaming Heights.

The eternity of the path does not intimidate it while the endlessness of the upcoming labour only serves to delight it.

It is the infinity of opportunities that leads it forward, revealing ever newer pages of spiritual creativity.

Aspire to follow a wonderful dream as though it were a guiding star, and know that the dream will be fulfilled sooner or later, depending upon the predestined periods involved.

Maintain your free will — free from all the mundane prejudices that would shackle it with fetters.

And create your deeds in the name of Love.

Advance through life, co-measuring your journey with Her alone.

She alone is capable of lending wings to your flaming spirit, which is capable of serving Her alone: Love — is a lodestar for your spirit.

8 December

A lark in the sky has heralded the beginning of the New Era, a stream has murmured about new currents, new leaves have unfolded, and new rays have permeated the renewed spheres, only man convulsively tries to hold on to the old, but it is already slipping out of his hands.

It is hard to hold back the decay and to turn rotten foundations into a reliable point of support.

All Nature is being imbued with new Fires, and eagerly inhaling the inflowing currents.

Breathe together with her, O man, if you want to see yourself as her crown.

And do not forget that I am not summoning you to dilate your nostrils, but to absorb the whole might of her healing rays through your heart.

And, when you have finally inhaled, do not forget to exhale them into the world around you so as to heat it by the warmth of your breath.

Breathe in... the Fire of the Heavens, breathe out... heartfelt Love.

Learn to breathe in a new way, and if you forget, the example of My birds will remind you.

A dream you have may enslave your consciousness, capturing it by contradictory feelings.

What lies in dreams, who writes their scripts, and who assigns you the role of the main character?

Such questions are hard for man to answer.

But I shall say that man himself is the only scriptwriter, skilfully working in the field of the unconscious.

Who else can penetrate the recesses of memory to make use of the installed material lying there under the heap of conglomerations, if the consciousness itself rarely knows what happens in the subconscious?

Look into yourself openly and honestly.

And let the dream become your good friend, pointing out shortcomings that ought to be thrown into the flame of transfiguration.

Peer into your dreams as you would into a mirror and do not draw a false portrait of yourself, when all the filthy evidence unfolds before your thought.

Dreams come to you only for purification.

PART II

Remember this, but not for the sake of excessive self-analysis, which only leads to self-disparagement.

You need to know yourself, and your dreams serve as your assistants in this.

Thought dominates the human nature.

It thrusts man into performing heroic deeds and pushes him to treachery.

And it is up to man himself to decide what thoughts he should cherish and what to cast away as unworthy of reflection.

But those who aspire to heroic deeds must grow heroic thoughts, for otherwise the seed of betrayal might end up in its place.

You should know what controls you, as this is your chief guide through life — your thought.

And do not forget that you are the one responsible for it.

If you have nothing, nothing can be taken from you.

And when you become rich — start giving to others on your own, without waiting until sufferers fall on their knees before you, begging for alms.

After all, wealth is given to test souls on their generosity.

But if you have no generosity, what can they possibly take from you?

"From one who has nothing, everything will be taken away, whereas to one who has everything, shall be given even more!"

How will you understand this truth?

And you must understand it and use it — otherwise you will have nothing to be taken away.

Apply this wisdom to yourself.

Seas and oceans surround dry land, but aerial bridges connect all the continents together, weaving them into a single pattern.

And so what if you are separated from someone when your thoughts intersect at a single point, bringing you much closer to each other.

You yourself know that you can be extremely distant from someone who is physically nearby; while no geographical distances can take away the feeling of closeness to another.

Nothing can separate: neither seas nor oceans, if hearts are connected by the currents of one Love.

The path spans the heights and is also laid out across the earth.

Who can tell whether one should follow the higher or the lower?

Of course, the road-builders have placed signs and markers to make their paths look more attractive.

PART II

And man must choose and not be deluded by the colours, knowing how magically attractive mirages can sometimes be.

Yet the heart will help select a simple path and will pave its own invisible pathway, not being enticed by the play of someone else's colours, even on the high roads.

The heart can take you away to the ultimate height; it knows the shortest passageways leading to the Divine Heights.

Trust the fiery heart — it will pave your way.

Is it fair to sling streams of mud at someone who, their Cup of Love filled to the brim, has descended to you from the Heavens in order to give drink to withered hearts?

Will it be justifiable to rain heavy stones upon open hearts?

And is it humane to shed false tears, when a High Spirit you have tormented steps over the borderline of Silence?

When a spark of life glimmers beside you and the Great Heart is beating, full of Love for you, all you need do is love.

Why is your love needed thousands of years after you indiscriminately crucified High Spirits by your own calumny?

They have gone from one life to another, trampled by human ignorance.

Why do you constantly look back?

After all, your eyes are not placed on the back of your head!

Look forward.

Look and see in clearer focus who it is that appears in front of you: people exhausted by the pain caused by your blindness!

When will you finally learn to appreciate the treasures the High Spirit brings you?

When will you stop killing those who bear the Cup of Love?

Neither by malice nor by hatred will you find salvation, but only by pure Love.

Only your loving heart will save you, for such is the Law of Heaven, and we cannot deny its justice.

9 December

It seems you can no longer get through the remaining section of the path.

But be aware that all tests are given in accordance with the level of your strength.

This too shall pass!

And you will overcome this, and one day you will look back with a bright smile, forever bidding farewell to the boundaries you have conquered.

PART II

And do not be afraid of something that has reared up before your eyes.

Remember: fear has enormous eyes.

But trust your heart and ask it for wise advice.

And, if you go through life with your hand upon the heart, so life will seem to you a marvellous fairy tale, and you will not even notice as the last segment of the path which seemed so unbearable falls into oblivion.

A leaf of My Garden is crying, watered with drops of silver rain.

It is mourning the fate of those who are trying to tear it off with their cold hands and trample it into the dirt.

Ah, this stardust — the Human Tribe!

How can they be made to realize that everyone is capable of being an enchanting orb, and the Creator wants to ignite a new star to fascinate the eyes of the entire Universe!

With the perishable and the Eternal on opposite pans of the scales, how can one choose decay and dust, when all of Nature is calling for Immortality?

But the choice is up to man — he must decide for himself.

And whether to drink from the Cup of Life or Death — that, too, is his own decision.

And they who have crumbled to dust will serve as food for new leaves that will cover the Garden with an emerald blanket, and the scattering of stars will sparkle on the drops of dew which cover them.

Minor servants of darkness are characterized by systematic retreat, but they still do not know which shore to aim for.

The ship is sinking, and it is pointless to be aboard, for it cannot withstand the powerful currents which are capturing all the elements.

And though they do not want to perish ingloriously, at the same time they cannot accept the path of salvation, for then they will have to admit their own defeat.

Unenviable is the fate of the apostates of either the Light or the darkness, for they who have betrayed the Fire have themselves cut off the path to salvation, while they who have deserted the darkness have evoked the bestial fury of gloom.

Will the soul craving the Light stand fast, and will it not fall even deeper into the dark abyss?

May courage never abandon it, and may it continue the struggle towards that boundary by whose crossing they will receive the right to assistance from the Forces of Light.

There is no more frightful battle than the one which takes place in the arena of your own soul.

And you need to triumph within, and establish the Banner of Light even more firmly than ever before.

To flee from the battlefield is contrary to the rules of My warriors: it is only after achieving a complete victory that they lay down their arms.

And none of them will run after to finish off the enemy or tread on the heels of their opponent.

In My Army there is no hatred, no feeling of revenge, no invasive thought.

We defend only what belongs to Us, according to the Law prescribed by the Heavens.

My warriors know no retreat, you must understand — they firmly hold the victorious Banner of Light, despite the formidable avalanche of the advancing enemy trying to knock them down — and the darkness *will* retreat.

I come when the old and the New must oppose one another on the battlefield.

I am not coming to reconcile them, but to cut off the enemy by a single stroke of My Fiery Sword, so that the seed of evil does not sink into the renewed soil.

We shall long have to cleanse the results of bloodstained steps and throw malignant spores into the flame.

But no one is able to delay the day of the final healing.

And in order to hasten the date of your spirit's liberation from its gloomy fetters, I shall walk through the Earth again.

Believe in yourself — in the Divine Powers of the human soul.

And may your faith spread through all Creation; then it will not be difficult for you to believe in My Advent.

Faith — this is your anchor, but do not break the mooring, for the raging elements will quickly break everything into matchwood.

Faith will save you — believe in this.

The complexity of the path consists in this: simple Truth is being rejected every hour, in whatever field of activity its light has sparkled.

But it cannot go on this way forever.

New people are coming and, being incarnated amidst the bowels of the grey mass which comprises the whole of humanity, they are starting to paint the world in different colours.

You cannot deny what is obvious to the earthly eye and step backwards, or tightly close your eyes beneath a shawl of ignorance.

Do not complicate the path for yourself, when I am saying that it can be extremely simple for you.

Look around: how clearly all Nature demonstrates the tone of transfiguration embracing her!

New winds are blowing, changing the focus of manifestation, and waters are rising heavenwards, born from melting glaciers.

And new clouds will settle as weightless oceans and seas, burying the layer of heavy waters beneath them.

And new lands will spring up, exposing themselves under cold ice, and their splendour of colours will amaze everyone as they thaw out human souls by their generous warmth.

I am calling you not to be the eyewitness of a miraculous transfiguration, but to become the co-creator of a New World, conceived in My currents.

Look around with fresh eyes and inhale something new every instant — in this way the Light of Transfiguration will touch you all the sooner, for in this New World must live new people!

10 December

Know, My children, that the Name of Maitreya is unshakeable through the ages.

Even thousands of names cannot eclipse it, for He is the Founding Father of the New Epoch and a starting-point, from which the Era of Love will commence and, as it becomes established, it will go through the whole Earth, embracing it with its fiery glow.

The Name of Maitreya is not for gossip; the Messenger of Maitreya is a blade scorched in the Fire.

Do not try to play with the Fire, knowing that it is endowed with the might of Maitreya.

The Flame of Divine Love is dominant throughout the infinite Universe, and there is nothing equal to the power of its currents.

You have nothing that can counteract or block the path of the Daughter of Fire, or attempt to come between Us or to cast up a lying word.

Our union is indissoluble, solemnized as it is by Eternity.

Do not joke with the Name of Maitreya.

I am a Defender of loving hearts.

You cannot go forward if you try taking the past along, but the future lends you its wings.

I have not come to gather death worms, but heavenly eagles who know the joy of flight.

Soar up to Flaming Heights, revealing your spirit in all its stellar beauty, and Infinity will be your House.

Strive to comprehend the incomprehensible, for only thus will you part with the past.

We judge by your deeds, not by your words, which pour out like a constant flood.

Fruitage is important to Us!

And We have seen enough of barren flowers.

PART II

Submit an idea to yourself and put it into practice in your life, and you will be rewarded according to your work.

This is how We shall judge.

The Reaper is coming upon a sown field, which is already plentiful with mature ears.

So what will He harvest if nothing has been sown?

What do you expect to obtain when you have neglected your field of activity, eroding the entire soil by the spores of poisonous thoughts?

Where shall We set up the Garden?

Where shall We cast Our seeds?

Consider this seriously; I am giving you the last instant to choose, holding out to you the cup of opportunities in full measure.

For the Great Love of you, the Reaper has descended, wishing to harvest Fires.

I shall say frankly so that you are under no illusions: the Flame is coming!

The Era of Love is not a myth and not a fairy tale.

Love is the Fire, the current of a supreme frequency.

If your conductors cannot withstand it, then everything will be incinerated in the blink of an eye.

Only spirituality — not feigned, but inner and genuine — will preserve your resiliency.

Faith in the Light, abiding in the heart — this is the powerful transmutator that will be able to assimilate the currents of salvation, exuding them into the surrounding world.

A loving heart alone will save you!

Remember what I have said.

Life makes heroes.

It weaves the daily pattern of your destiny, it co-ordinates actions and monitors the quality of your thoughts.

Life will correct the direction of your progression, only hear it without succumbing to the instigation of death, which is always ready to broadcast its instructions.

Listen sensitively and contrast the voice of the "rational" mind with the wisdom of the heart — it wishes to see you as a hero, and you will become such.

Love always must be the main argument, provided this concept is applicable.

Love justifies everything, if your deeds are done in her name.

Do not go against her and do not rule her out when you put forward various thoughts.

Learn to think through the Light of Love, then all your problems will be resolved.

And know that Love will never condemn, but will always justify.

My Judge is beautiful and incorruptible.

Give your destiny into Her Hands.

And follow those Laws that are prescribed by Sacred Love.

Heavenly Bliss will enter your life, if you do not lose the most important quality of your heart — the ability to love!

11 December

The Empyreal Land is all in motion: Maitreya is coming!

His steps resound through all the spheres, embracing all the Seven Planes of Existence.

There is no death for Maitreya, just as there are no borders between the visible and invisible worlds: all is one, all in all.

The Time of Maitreya is limitless, He is beyond any restrictions of Time and Space.

The period allotted to Him by the Plan of Cosmic Evolution is infinite.

Maitreya is the Fire, pouring out as a broad flow all over your world.

It will fill the whole Earth.

And the transforming Flame will pervade all hearts, and they will eternally glorify the One who has brought them the Light of Liberation.

Welcome the Lord of the Empyreal World, for His steps are already heard in your world.

The caressing Sun enkindles fires every day and gives them away with ever-growing generosity.

A great example is revealed to you.

And I wish to name each of you My little sun, warm and gentle.

And I shall so name you, if you multiply the fire of your heart, which increases immeasurably as a result of your magnanimous giving.

Show your endearing currents through your daily movements.

Before My Advent, you noticed a special invigoration of the forces of Nature.

They have revealed the Power of Life, after receiving the impetus of new currents.

I shall not leave the world until Truth is affirmed.

My Truth is — Love!

I have come to you only to affirm it.

The planet will shudder in a gigantic cataclysm, but you will not even notice this, being captivated by the contemplation of smaller and fragmented natural calamities.

PART II

All the Forces of Light have been enlisted to save the integrity of the planetary body.

And this last cataclysm, brought on by the forces of darkness, will come crashing down upon themselves, forever burying them under the heavy debris of the old world.

And I shall repeat once again that this will not be visible to the earthly eye; however, your heart will feel the moment of the final Victory, and you will experience an instant of liberation in spirit.

The entire hierarchy of darkness will collapse, after being fundamentally shattered from the moment they lost their leader.

The Fire will purify the world, burning all the remains in huge bonfire sites.

The planet will be saved — I have given you My word!

A great feast is celebrated.

The voice of angelic trumpets has already announced the victory achieved on the Ethereal Planes.

But the minions of the darkness are bustling, hatching invasive plans deep down in the netherworld.

Although they know that the Light never retreats from positions conquered in the heat of battle, they are nevertheless still zealously recruiting fellow-fighters, choosing blind minions from the thick of the human mass.

And shallow earthlings willingly succumb to them, and for a while they even manage to capture the minds of those who are striving to follow the path of Light.

They meekly carry out the will of the darkness, hiding behind the mask of their "devotion to the purity of the Teachings."

Even if it is possible to fool dozens or hundreds of people in this way, it is absolutely impossible to mislead Us by demonstrating a false zeal in their serving.

One who serves the Sacred Fire does not discuss the Teachings, but silently carries out their commands.

Discard pointless arguments and forsake those who are not able to hear the voice of the heavenly trumpets announcing the Victory of My warriors.

My warriors are not the kind who try to win disputes, but their destiny is to win in battle by the light in their hearts, which are full of Love for their enemies.

Are those who vomit up condemnations right?

"No, of course not," you will answer.

Then why do you yourselves disparage your fellow-beings?

Condemnation is dangerous in itself, but disparagers cannot even imagine what a dreadful avalanche their tongue evokes when they attempt to disparage the children of the Divine Fire.

A condemning word has a boomerang effect: what you utter will not only return to you, but it will strike you with multifold force.

Will you manage to stand fast?

Think about it!

And do not say you are coming to Me — I do not recognize anyone coming to Me with a poisonous sting, for I cannot abide forked tongues.

Whether one of My children is right or wrong is not for you to judge, but for Me.

And this is the whole truth, as affirmed by Life.

The wind will disperse ashes and fertilize new soil.

Self-reviving and self-regenerating matter is revealed in the world.

But how can you detect and register it by your devices when you have no such devices?

The New Era brings also new discoveries, and each one will be offered to a seeking spirit who at the right time shows their devotion to renewable science.

All sources of Knowledge have been given to the Earth, and many constitute inexhaustible wells, but the reservoirs of priceless treasures lie deep.

It is necessary to develop them and thoroughly loosen the compressed soil; for hidden under its layers lies Truth.

Rise from the ashes, for you already possess this power, even if you are not aware of it.

Currents are weaving different patterns of life.

And you should not approach them with old yardsticks, attempting to measure something that is not subject to measurement.

Think in a new way, and the entire beauty of newness will be revealed to you in the great simplicity of discoveries which your spirit will make.

Only by filling your thoughts with the fiery substance will you succeed in making a breakthrough in your study of matter, which conceals the forces of Life.

And remember that you will comprehend the Science of Fire only when your heart masters the self-regenerating currents.

Resurrection — is not a fairy tale for superstitious old ladies, but a fact that you can prove scientifically.

12 December

We relax restrictions, calling it *Tactica Adversa*.

Otherwise, how shall We understand what any given creature is capable of, if their field of activity is limited?

If We place a bird in a cage, how can We possibly determine what heights it is capable of soaring to?

PART II

Only absolute freedom will provide the true knowledge about whatever creature We are testing.

That is why We say that you must act according to your *free will*.

We do not force anything upon anyone; neither do We impose restrictive limits on anybody.

We wish to see your spirit as a free bird in the sky, and that is why We ease restrictions in everything.

A product of the mind is not always edible.

No matter how much adornment you apply, a corpse is always a corpse.

Distinguish a living thought from a dead one.

Ask your heart: it knows the measure of distinction and never errs.

However, the impatient scream of the rational mind is always attempting to muffle the barely audible, silent voice of the heart.

And how can you hear Silence?

Is it possible?

I say: Yes, it is!

You need only calm down the race of chaotic thoughts and strain your ears.

And if the thought you heard was full of Love, then it came from the heart.

But if it had the cold feel of rationality, it was the product of the mind.

Whether you are doing right or wrong, this is not for Me to decide — but for you.

You choose your own path and make decisions for yourself.

Whatever will it be: the higher or the lower, the light or the dark, with Me or without Me — you are responsible for your own choice!

But first answer to yourself: to whom are you going?

And, if you are treading a path into the darkness and defiling all My shrines along your way, do not say that you are hurrying towards Me.

No roads towards Me are paved with fanaticism or superstition, persecution or condemnation.

The path towards Me is paved with Love and, if advancing souls leave a bright deed in their wake, allowing those following to shine even brighter, it means they have chosen the higher path.

There are no threats, no condemnations in My breast: someone else's will is sacred and none of Us will intervene in an ongoing attempt to recruit them to Our side.

But, having said the choice is yours, We only warn you that those who have chosen the darkness are heading towards death, whereas those yearning for the Light are advancing towards Immortality.

PART II

And whether you are making the right or the wrong choice is up to you to decide.

But I must remind you once more of your responsibility for your choice before the Law of Cosmic Evolution.

The Earth can be called a launch pad: from here the human spirit launches deep into the Infinite Ocean, bestrewn with twinkling stars.

The correctness of the flight trajectory depends upon a good start; so does maintaining lasting resiliency under extreme conditions and, ultimately, the achievement of the goal.

And now We see a soul approaching the edge of an abyss, driven there by a frenzied Human Race.

And, having given away her generous and imperishable gifts, she casts a final glance at the infuriated faces, covering them with a seal of heartfelt Love.

Then, with one final effort, she gently ascends to the vault of heaven, where she sets herself up as a bright little star with the sole aim of pouring Love eternally upon everything around her, looking into the eyes of her persecutors, as though asking: "When will you stand beside me?"

Look, people, how much space there still is within the Stellar Ocean!

Prepare for the start and give birth to a new star!

Plagiarism is to be condemned.

But will it be plagiarism, if thousands of different peoples suddenly begin to give voice to the same idea that has dawned upon them?

And if identical masterpieces are born in different corners of the world, and a single melody resounds throughout the realm of music, and paintings everywhere reflect similar colours — will not this be evidence that they have drawn their inspiration from a common source?

I give a common language to the world — the language of Love.

And if all begin to speak it, affirming the single thought of Divine Love through all their domains of activity, plagiarism will completely disappear, losing its meaning even as a concept.

Time will compress; one spiral will join another and merge into a single Round.

The Periods will be established all over the world.

They will rule human life.

And everyone will understand and accept the Law of Cyclicity in the development of all Creation, but they will take it far beyond the limits defined by Time.

The Universe lives by different norms, outside the concepts of *Time* and *Space*.

Man is a cosmic creature, and he is to live according to the Laws of the Cosmos prescribed from birth.

PART II

Bravely enter the New Round, realizing the untimely demise of the old time.

The borders of ages are being erased, and thousands of years are being compressed into a single point.

How far has man gone in his development?

However, in terms of the inner plane, you are not so far from your cave ancestors.

Yes, you have developed the brain, there is no question.

But what has your mind led you to, while your heart remains so underdeveloped?

So sophisticated have you become in inventions, reaching a level of "high art" in methods of killing each other.

You have atrophied the heart, making it a bloody organ composed of muscles.

But you forgot that your souls were sent to the Earth not for the heart to serve as an appendage of the mind, but so that the mind might fully obey the heart.

And only when the flaming heart adorns the altar of your soul, brimming over with Divine Love, only then can you consider yourself a Man created in the image of God.

See whether you might not have been overtaken by animals, who have stepped upon the first rung of cordiality much earlier than their human counterparts!

Ponder the heart seriously, filling your thought therewith.

The salvation of the world is within your hearts.

Not only are the borders of ages being effaced, but those that have entrenched themselves in the Human Kingdom without climbing to a higher rung will be erased from the face of the Earth.

Neither can they be established midst animals or flowers, for even there the currents of Sacred Love are starting to dominate.

From soulless stone they will begin their evolution once again, and if they fail to make a step forward, they will crumble to dust and provide food for new flowers.

Create Man from yourself, O man — for the path of God is outlined for you!

13 December

Pain abates and wounds close through a kind word spoken from the heart.

You do not come to multiply afflictions, both yours and others, but to heal the whole world by the beauty of good deeds, forgetting about the pain that torments your heart day and night.

Advance from words to deeds.

Move from your warm spot — an airliner can only be tested in flight, not in a hangar, where it stands immovable.

PART II

The sky, not the earth, tests its flight qualities.

And no matter how vigorously hens flap their wings, they cannot fly higher than their roost.

That is why I say unto birds of short-distance flight: do not attempt to teach My eagles how to soar, but work on your own wings so that they might be able to lift your unliftable bodies.

Divert yourself from the mundane, only not in words but in acts, for We judge according to your deeds rather than words.

My warriors stand like a granite cliff.

They know that they are posted on guard, and they will not leave their post unless they receive an order which resounds within their heart.

The house of the spirit is strong, and there is no doubt that My warriors' feet will not stumble as they step upon shaky earthly soil and, like a giant cliff, they will stand fast, defending those who will find the peace of salvation in the shadow of their backs.

Be aware, people, that the time of the Last Angel has come and the voice of his trumpet will herald the fall of the darkness and the triumph of the Kingdom of God's Light.

And the slumberers will awake and the dead will rise, not a single soul will remain who has not heard the Heavenly Voice.

And those who have heard it, will make the final choice, revealing the seal of either the darkness or the radiating Light on their forehead.

Know, people, that when the Last Angel's trumpet sounds, it will be too late to make the choice.

What can you possibly find new for yourself in attempting to sort out someone else's squabbles?

How many pearls do you think you can find in the garbage when you know what the waste consists of?

Do not spoil the purity of your consciousness by cluttering and defiling the chastity of the source.

Better listen to the heart, to its silent voice, and it will present you with a thought of extraordinary beauty.

Merge with it in a simple conversation and make it your natural interlocutor, then your treasury will be brimming over with new pearls every day.

You need to discern My Word.

Everything is simple and accessible to the human consciousness.

I am speaking with you in the most simple language you can possibly find, endeavouring to touch all the innermost strings of your soul.

Will you resonate?

I do not know that.

However, I know one thing: you will always hear Me, if you are only willing to tune your ear to the sensitive perception of all My Words.

But keep in mind — a lot of what is said to the heart might not be accessible to the mind, even though I am expressing My Word extremely simply.

Sing along with Me the Song of Heroic Deeds which has been generated by the Light of Love.

Your heart knows this melody, for I Myself placed it there at the moment you descended into earthly flesh.

The dominant note in the world is born — it is the Note of Love.

And only by its sound will you recognize each other.

The Army of Maitreya advances by Love, triumphing in Her Name and glorifying Her by singing the Song of Heroic Deeds.

14 December

The fulfilment of a dream depends upon you alone, upon the quality of your aspirations.

And if they are pure, then I shall add My might to them, and all, even the most fabulous, will come true.

Give yourself a chance to soar up like a bird and proudly open wide your wings, with no fear of heights.

And, upon reaching boundless heights, give yourself a chance to soar even higher, for the Flaming Heights are unlimited.

Know everything you are interested in.

Do not live by prohibitions; for if you do, you will never know flight.

Only the thought of freedom will direct you heavenwards and open your vision to stellar expanses.

What can be forbidden for a star?

What can defile it?

Nothing is able to even come close to the Flame that can tarnish it or take away its chastity — anything like that will be burnt by the Fire, incinerated in an instant.

Go forward freely, putting no blinders on your eyes.

Lift up your head and take a royal look around the whole world: here everything belongs to you.

You are the creator.

And the creator must know everything.

The purity of My children is irreproachable.

The earthly world judges by external man, whereas the Empyreal judges by the heart ablaze with the Fire.

I do not try to compare one with the other, for I know that the former, having been born from ashes, will return to ashes, mingling with filth and dust.

PART II

The latter, on the other hand, will make a flaming ascent to the Fiery Heights, adorning the vault of heaven with yet another bright, bright star, whose chastity and purity will eternally attract attention.

The past and the future are incompatible, even though they intersect at one point, named *the present*.

It is here that one dies and the other originates — hence, it can also be called the point of Life and Death.

I welcome the death that serves for the sake of the resurrection and the triumph of Life; I do not accept the life which exudes a deathly stench.

The "living dead" are not fiction; they are among you.

Do not infect yourself with the spores of decomposition; you should know that the post-mortem poison they emit is quite dangerous.

Love alone is capable of neutralizing it.

And because of this, I say: Protect yourself!

It is impossible to go forward while looking backwards, or to live the way the dead "live."

Let them remain in the past for you.

Turn away and strive to eternally advance into the future with a single aspiration.

Walk in such a way that all those who follow you will be delighted by the trace you left in the past.

Let yourself now rest, having tamed the run of chaotic thoughts.

Like voracious worms, they are ready to devour you from inside.

Do not then pander to such insatiable creatures but put up a protective barrier against them, shielding yourself from absolute death by the power of pure prayer.

If you sow densely the thought of Joy, you will be rewarded a thousandfold.

I prefer to see a human being as a whole fruit, showing forth both internal and external beauty.

Do not get involved in thoughts of self-devouring, as self-torment comes from the darkness.

Rest from these "labours," so grave and gloomy, and arm yourself with at least one healing thought: May the Light of Love shine forth in resurrection!

And you yourself will be resurrected from it, I assure you.

The path is complicated, but also beautiful!

You have to pay for everything, and you should not forget that everyone pays with the coin they have.

And Love alone can be the measure of your payment, My children, and no matter how they try to deceive you, do not mint false coins in response or attempt to reckon with an offender, or you will end up owing even more.

Cover your debt with Love, and to those who owe you much forgive much; in this way you will avoid complicating the path both for yourself and for them.

Love cannot be lent, and interest from it does not accrue.

Pay honestly, with all your heart realizing that it is your duty to pay for everything with Love.

I have pointed out to you a complicated path, but there is none more beautiful, for it is extremely simple in its essence.

15 December

I affirm a bright moment of Illumination within every heart that has heard My Call.

Be silent, O ye deaf, shout not, O ye sleepers — you do not know the sound of My Voice, for you have already overslept your life.

And do not try to put to mortal sleep those who have been touched by the gift of insight.

Be careful with the Flame that has blazed up within hearts, for it possesses omnipotent power.

If you go against the Fire which brings the Light of Insight to good souls, you might end up incinerating yourselves.

So-called malevolent fate only *seems* to be malevolent.

Look at things through different eyes, gazing from the opposite pole.

And under the prism of Light, everything will take on different colours, and then you will glorify your destiny, which has brought you so much good.

Look at things through the lens of kindness, for an evil gaze will try to daub everything in spiteful hues.

And so paint your destiny in that colour which is closest to you.

No one needs flattery; as a quality generated by the darkness, it only spoils.

Those who listen to silken adulation with obvious satisfaction are imperceptibly slipping down the high ladder they earlier conquered through incredible effort.

Flattery is alien to everyone who follows the path of Light, yet it can inflate the self-satisfaction of the servants of darkness, who float up like soap bubbles, shimmering in a splash of colours.

So, do not be allured by the false light and do not adulate the obesity of inflation, for excessive feeding may only burst this bubble, leaving people with nothing but a sense of deep disappointment.

No two people are alike, and so do not judge on the basis of a single individual.

PART II

Become sensitive to individual human souls, paying special attention to how each one reacts to the adulation surrounding them.

The power of money is enormous for someone who has put themselves in slavish dependence on money.

But it has no authority over My child, who is soaring as a free bird over the entire mundane vanity.

There is no purpose for man lower than the one involving the accumulation of monetary stock.

Why build houses of cards when they are unsuitable for living?

Imperishable treasures must be accumulated in the spirit.

Work brightly for their multiplication, and everything else will follow, even the material.

The Flame is coming!

All the Ethereal Spheres are already enveloped in the invisible Fire.

And the domains of the Fire are broadening, already advancing throughout earthly expanses.

This unified Flame will penetrate all worlds, burning all the boundaries between the lowest and the highest, between countries and peoples, between the past and the future, leaving nothing in the world that brings separation.

The Epoch of Unity has begun, and the Flame will unite all of you who are proceeding with Love in your hearts.

It is important to overcome your lower self.

And the need to establish authority over your lower bodies is urgent as never before.

You cannot allow them to rule over the supreme, for a shepherd is placed over the herd, and not the other way round.

Appreciate the sheer pricelessness of your stellar spirit and make it your shepherd, subjecting even the basest aspects of yourself to it.

You yourself know what happens to a herd of sheep when it is left unattended.

It will be hard to gather the stray lambs, and you will not be able to rescue those that fall prey to a wolf's teeth.

Save yourself before it is too late, and try to establish a unified integrity; this is achieved only by overcoming yourself.

There is no future in the Future for those who have rejected it.

It exists only for those who have carefully constructed it, paving the way with faith and hope.

The Future is delightfully beautiful, for it has been built not over the course of a year or two, but over long millennia, and all of humanity's most marvellous dreams have been used in its construction.

I have come to the Earth to establish your brightest aspirations.

16 December

Gird yourself in the Name of the Lord Maitreya as an impenetrable armour.

A sense of invulnerability will come over you, along with an unwavering confidence in His might, protecting you from malicious and poisonous earthly arrows.

The Name of Maitreya will provoke vehement attacks on the part of the darkness, yet it will vehemently protect you from them.

Do not attach so much importance to the eccentricities of someone else's character, for this can greatly delay you on your path.

Character changes slowly, and you should not match yourself to its pace.

It is better to pay attention to the opportunities of your spirit, and only on the basis of its deeds should you judge another, yet not with condemnation, but only justification.

And with the skilful use of its features, you can put a person's character to your service, imperceptibly changing it so as to make it much better than before.

Experienced pianists know all the qualities of their instrument.

And they will not play it or attempt to elicit harmonious sounds from it unless the strings are properly tuned.

They know that the instrument must be first tuned, bringing each string into a single unison.

And then a wonderful melody will pour out, if the right note is struck.

But what can a man produce, if he is all upset and his nerves are already beginning to snap one after another, like taut strings?

You have come not to produce falsity, but to show the world the marvellous song of your soul.

This is why I say: Come to yourself, O man, as an experienced tuner, so that I might call you a great pianist — one who has delighted the Divine Ear of the Creator of the Worlds with the melody of your flaming spirit.

My dear, beloved children of the Earth!

Why are you in anguish, why do you call out only to perdition in trying to save yourselves from all the misfortunes crowding around?

Have not I provided you with the right means — a means that will restore to Life?

PART II

Death will not help your soul, but the Light of Love, reborn within your hearts, will help you overcome all troubles.

And again I say unto you: There are no stronger or mightier currents than those of Divine Love; they hold sway over all the worlds, and they alone will overcome your anguish, My dear children of the Earth.

Do not make yourself a prisoner.

Do not seek out golden cages, for they are disastrous for free birds.

You will find not comfort, but deathly anguish, which is worthless to sing about, no matter how well they feed you in your cramped cage.

Find freedom and sing an unfettered song, so that from its sounds the walls of dungeons collapse, releasing all prisoners to the light of the Sun.

Play is not always fun, especially when those who instigate it do not know how to play.

There are things which many of you should not touch at all.

Do not become the subject of other people's fun, for you will end up with a sad finale.

Let those have fun who have already gone mad, incessantly inciting amusement; but you should remember what the time is like that you are living in now, and realize that soon nobody will be having any fun at all.

The avalanche of the Fire will cover the world, but it will be invisible.

Love will pour out in a broad flow, but She will be visible to hearts alone.

The Lords will reveal their Faces to you, but only your spirit will be able to recognize them.

My Flame is touching you, but still you are averting your eyes.

You will not be able to avoid the evidence that will be manifest to your gaze.

And for those who are spiritually blind there is no place in My World, where only those who have sighted hearts can live.

17 December

The affairs of the darkness are in a bad way; despite all the rage it pours forth, the process of destruction has turned against it.

One cannot destroy someone else's structures — or one will end up encroaching upon one's own.

The darkness has many servants, in addition to a host of minions ready to oblige.

Yet, to counteract it, the Armada of Light is increasing and flaming hearts are starting to blaze!

In contrast to the darkness, We succeed not through quantity but through quality.

PART II

And only one warrior of Mine is able to withstand the onslaught of the entire demonic host.

Examples of this are many, and they are multiplying everywhere.

I say this not to scare you and not for your edification: they who come with the darkness are doomed to perdition, for its works are evil.

Enough monasteries have already been built.

You will not seclude yourselves, but unite when My Advent occurs.

It is easy to love people when you fence yourselves off from them by a monastery wall, but it is extremely difficult when you are in the midst of a crowd.

The Saviour walked through crowds surrounding Him like a wall, and danger threatened Him from all sides, yet He did not hide even from His persecutors, but His loving heart was aimed directly at them, for they knew not what they were doing.

And you who are robed in priestly cassocks, do you know what you are doing when you persecute those who are marked with His high seal?

For the persecutors of Love, there is no place in the Eternal Kingdom, and monastery walls will not protect, for they will crumble once they have outlived their usefulness.

What will you cover your spiritual bareness with?

Give serious thought to your own situation and, instead of building on the sand, erect a temple within your heart, unfenced by walls...

Except for that living wall which will surround you and bow before your spirit: the Human Race is often grateful, even though it may come too late.

Yet this is not a disaster.

Serve the Human Kingdom, embracing it with your immeasurably increasing Love, whose generous currents you may use to encircle it like a monastery wall so as to ardently preserve the spirit of sacredness.

The march of the Sun begins in the East, while the sunset is awaited by the West — this is determined by the forces of Nature.

Do not expect an ardent flourishing of the Fire where its ascent is not designated, for a spirit of extinction hovers over everything.

And always direct your gaze towards the East, for that is where the Sun arises — the new Orb of the Spirit ascending to the zenith of His Fiery Glory.

Maitreya is advancing, leaving Fiery Tushita in order to establish its Light through all the worlds which abide in the darkness.

All spheres — both earthly and Empyreal — will be dwelling places for Gods: for He comes to make Gods out of you.

Rely on yourself — during a long journey anything can happen: you might not find something you need close by, or a friendly hand reaching out to you, or who knows what else.

After all, it is indeed hard to make your shouts heard amidst the deaf.

You have to count on your own forces alone.

This is why I say: rely upon yourself.

And you will find the strength to overcome all circumstances within yourself — it is within your spirit.

I love independent aspirants — remember this!

I release a flock of birds into wide open expanses.

Each of them will compose their song, revealing to the world the beauty of heavenly sounds.

But be careful, My children, when your feet touch earthly soil, for there are still many snares set for free-flying birds.

Preserve in your hearts a never-ending aspiration to soar to the heights — this is something inherent in the spirit of the bird.

As you raise fledgelings, inculcate in them a thirst for freedom, and release them in flight, thereby multiplying My flock of swans, preserving in their faithful hearts the Song of Love; and may all expanses be filled with this Song.

Try to write a poem or a simple verse about Love.

Where will you draw inspiration from if you feel empty inside, and the emptiness around you resounds with but a hollow echo?

But if your soul is full of longing and your world is filled with living sounds, the touch of which transfixes your trembling heart, trust Me: lines will flow out all by themselves, and you need only write them down.

Look attentively into the world and, standing still, listen to what is happening in the depths of your breast: there a poet is emerging!

Love brings forth Creators, and she creates geniuses.

Try to set on a pedestal at least a few simple words, stringing lines together like beads, dedicating them to Ethereal Love, and you will take a huge step forward, proceeding from mortal man towards Immortal God.

18 December

Poles are shifting, and everything in the world is beginning to change with catastrophic speed.

People cannot keep pace with the seven-league strides of Nature — that is why so many disasters befall them.

You need to hurry if you want to find that knowledge which has been placed into your treasure — for therein lies your salvation.

PART II

Move away from the dead point and take a look at all things from the polar opposite viewpoint that before had been foreign to you; perhaps, then, Truth will be closer to you than ever.

The most accessible understanding to man is that which he can behold with his earthly eyes.

However, not all things are subject to examination, as many remain beyond the limits of the visible.

It is in these things that the cause of various phenomena lies hidden.

To penetrate with your eyes beyond the border of the invisible is an urgent task, in which only the human heart can help you.

You must understand that its possibilities are boundless; indeed, it will bring you closer to the comprehension of all Creation.

Connections are established between countries and peoples.

So what is next?

Next you need to lift your head and look closely into the infinite Stellar Ocean.

Why do you deny a connection with the Supreme Worlds?

Why does this connecting fall to the very few people capable of co-operation with the Empyreal Land?

Are We not willing to establish friendly relations?

A mass of evidence is revealed by Our constant attempts to consolidate the connections between the two worlds: the physical and the Subtle.

We were and still are among you, why will you not pay a visit to Us?

Let us look at things through different eyes: they surround us for two reasons.

First, we brought them close to ourselves, by our will; and second, they were imposed upon us by someone else's will.

What things are the closest and most precious for you?

Should you not get rid of something that oppresses you and leave only what makes you happy?

Note that all things, like all people, are capable of carrying the energy of evil or good placed in them.

Thus some will bring you peace and harmony, while others offer only irritation and a feeling of devastation, for, like vampires, they can suck out your life forces.

Look around you and carefully consider whether you live among friends or enemies.

And if you abhor your environment, you can change it, and look at all things through different eyes.

PART II

For those who bear the Light of Love, let us find a most honourable place and erect a snow-white altar within our heart.

Yet let us not revere them with our mind, surrounding them with empty and idle words, but with our entire soul, full of great gratitude towards them.

Words are an empty sound if heartfelt currents are not applied; it is better to keep silent than to vibrate space with husks vociferously thrown at the Bearer of the Supreme Light.

I shall not vanish like smoke, and I shall not fly by as a breath of wind.

I shall embrace the whole world in the currents of My Love, and you will breathe them, for they will infuse all space.

The seal of Maitreya's Sacred Love will begin to shine like a star upon everyone's forehead, revealing the fiery-white core.

And My Flaming Face will always accompany you, protecting you with the Shield of Love from the slightest whiff of malice.

I have come to melt the cold and to dissolve in the Fire of Love all the lumps of ice created by cold human indifference.

And I assure you that cold human hearts, once touched by My warmth, will thaw out, and I shall abide within them forever.

I shall not allow My warriors to hang their heads.

It is always possible to find a solution in any circumstances — there are no hopeless situations — you only need discover the right decision.

And, of course, a kind heart will help you in this endeavour, provided that you have not weak-mindedly placed it under the executioner's axe, which he might let drop without thinking.

But do give it your thoughtful consideration and call upon pure Heaven, accompanying your appeal not with screams of horror and despair, but with a bright prayer of the heart.

And a solution will arrive, and a thought of salvation will appear, only listen to it, and it will release you from any possible trap.

Solve the problems of life wisely, the way they are solved in fairy tales, and victory will be yours.

Lift up your head and go forward confidently, stepping forth like a hero.

You are proceeding together with Me, and the entire might of the Hierarchy is at your back, vigilantly and joyously following the victorious steps of the warrior of Light.

PART II

19 December

New ideas will arrive — do not discard them, and despite any seeming absurdity, try to find a grain of reason.

From inspiration to a discovery is but a single step, so do take it and multiply the imperishable riches of the world, imbuing it with the light of the new idea revealed.

Many beliefs are based upon facts that can actually be proved scientifically, though they may be but fragments of the whole veil of Truth.

And their deep roots have been preserved and are frozen in anticipation of the miracle of regeneration.

A flower pressed in a book reveals little about its stalk and the roots which nourished it, but you cannot deny them, for how was the flower brought to the light in the first place?

A lot of things lie hidden amidst both oral and written legends, reflected within tightly fitted lines.

And behind each of them is concealed a grain that gave life to a particular phenomenon.

But once you finish digging to the root, you will reach a truth that does not require proofs, for it is obvious beyond a shadow of a doubt.

THE CALL OF THE HEART

Tempestuous winds are subsiding, and they are peacefully toning down their ardour, having completed the work assigned them by the Forces of Evolution.

The elemental forces have a lot of work to do at the borders of transitional Epochs.

And how else to reach out to living creatures immersed in centuries-old dreams?

They cannot bury the sleeping!

At the same time they need to awake, swirling everything around as in a whirlwind, and they need to give a push to people's backs so that the accompanying current might provide them with fresh forces.

Everything is placed at the service of man, he needs only to understand that creative power presented to him by the more rambunctious elements.

And once they come together in gentle co-operation, all the mighty winds will abate, obediently moderating their temper and demonstrating meekness in their service.

A marvellous lotus flower will blossom within the breast and endow the world with magical colours, dazzling everyone with its beauty.

Yes, many cannot withstand the invisible Light radiated by an all-loving heart, and they will be blinded by their own fury, incapable of accepting the currents of Love.

PART II

Others, by contrast, having touched the long-awaited warmth, will close their eyes to all the vanity manifest in the world; they will make themselves blind and reject what had attracted their gaze before.

The lotus of the heart is unfolding the All-Seeing Eye of Love, granting access to the vision of all the Divine Worlds.

And whoever wishes to see them must go blind and turn away from the mundane, then, becoming sighted, turn to the Heavenly, unfolding all the petals of the marvellous fiery flower which blossoms in the trembling breast.

Once each century, We issue a Message, filling the world but once with the Call of Our Hearts.

Who will respond?

Who will resound and emit a blissful sound from the strings of their heart?

The negligibly small number of hearts lit up like candles from the Fire brought to them are immediately faced with attacks by those who do not accept the Divine Light.

It is not just that they will be surrounded with a solid ring by the servants of the darkness, but poisonous arrows will fly into their backs from sources least expected.

Thus those who have responded with their *mind* then begin to persecute those whose *hearts* have accepted Our Light; being essentially good people, they attempt to take over the role of the supreme leader, running ahead and preaching to their fellows who are bearing heavy crosses.

Do not touch those who are walking with unbearable loads, and unless you are ready to share them, remove yourselves from the road and do not flit like annoying flies before their eyes.

The Call is sounding!

Tame your garrulous tongues and let your sensitive hearts listen closely to My Voice, which is speaking right this very moment.

The Light is coming from the East!

Every century is filled with Our Call, and Our Oriental age — in contrast to the Western century — is characterized by a cycle of sixty years.

And if you once already missed hearing the resounding Call, try to catch it now, as it is sounding for the last time at the crossing of Ages.

We are issuing the Message to the heart — understand — to the *heart*!

Day passes in vanity and feuds, however, the Light of Illumination will flash in the blaze of day, full of the bright call of Love.

PART II

It calls you to pure tranquillity, to the clear sky warmed by the solar light.

Turn your gaze to the unfathomable heights and understand, O man, how worthless is the vanity with which you have surrounded yourself, and how pointless are the feuds which you start every day.

Why do you kill all the bright possibilities which Heaven bestows upon you, knowing that each new day is a rung that allows you to rise higher?

Take care of the Sun, O man — the Sun of the new day!

The warmth of the Fire is enveloping the planet: glaciers are dissolving, the earthly firmament is melting and even human flesh is thawing, rarefying its structure that has become so stale during its long passage traversing the earthly path.

Everything will become lighter and purer, owing to the currents which are permeating the whole world.

You will find the signs of new transformations everywhere: they are all in plain sight, yes, and even within you.

Listen to yourself — and you will discover new bright phenomena clearly occurring in the recesses of your breast.

The human heart is awakening, blazing up like the dawn over your entire lived life, as well as throughout the life you are to live eternally!

The Fire is coming!

It will awake the Chalice of knowledge, it will open the treasure of your spirit, and it will spread wide your flaming wings.

You are a creator.

Create a map of the New World with pure thoughts, remembering that you are to live on a planet which is being renewed in everything.

20 December

The world will finally awaken and, having being awakened by the sound of the bell ringing within each heart, it will not be able to fall asleep again.

The long and gloomy night is approaching its end, and it is impossible to prolong it, no matter how hard its servants try.

The ray of the Sun will disperse the darkness, and the Light will accede to the throne, establishing the Epoch of Wise Insight.

Wake up, O man, and look around you: the whole world is waiting just for your awakening, as all the forces of Nature have already been roused.

It is not at all difficult to put this into practice, if you immediately consider and adopt the final decision within yourself.

PART II

But if you simply agree with the rightness of the words and then let them float in one ear and out the other, it is hardly probable that they will be put into practice in any specific instance.

Hence, if possible, you should put it into practice right away; this will allow you to develop the needed determination which will always result not in words, but in lightning-fast actions.

Many earthly expanses are powdered with snow, and the white covering has again reminded you of the purity of thought.

Man's destructive thought corrodes the earth's crust, devastating and exterminating its luxuriant vegetation.

The "two-legged thinkers" are ready to cover the world with lifeless deserts; however, snow has put obstacles in their path, using its whiteness to cover places which it will win back for only one purpose: to grow white gardens.

Why not arm yourself with a similar thought, and thus help adorn the earthly expanses?

Is it not enough to cram your eyes with dust and sand?

Is it not better to grow the tree of knowledge within the heart and to embroider your thought, unfolding it as a snow-white flower?

THE CALL OF THE HEART

Thus you will save both yourself and a world which is reaching out for purity of thought.

Think pure thoughts and weave a pattern of deeds like a crystal snowflake, bringing the bliss of healing to all Creation.

The ray's speed of movement is equal to the speed of the thought that gave it birth.

You need only think about a particular person to touch them immediately with the ray of reminiscence, highlighting all the various aspects of them you remember.

A negative attitude will tinge all your thoughts with gloomy tones, and a clot of negative energies will fly along the ray, striking a heavy blow; whereas a pure transmission will glide along like a solar arrow, breaking through the barriers of the darkness once constructed between you.

You should not think evil — not only out of fear that someone will pass along your words and strike a blow: you have already struck one through your thought if you have touched someone with a trenchant ray — even for a single instant.

Remember the speed of thought and skilfully control its rays, which carry the gift of healing.

Rely on the Will of God and do not attempt to set the paltry against the supreme, for you do not wish to

PART II

prevent the Creator from showing forth a better pattern of your destiny than you could ever have imagined.

He knows the best solution, for all the threads of Karma are gathered in His Hands.

And some knots will be untwined, while others will not be tied at all, and once you gain your freedom, your destiny, woven as it is from the pattern of stellar threads, will not take long to offer you its gifts.

And do not entrust yourself to earthly spiders, which are always ready to catch you in a web, but put your trust in Heaven, relying in everything upon the Will of the Almighty.

Look at yourself!

Are you satisfied with what you behold?

And if you are not happy with the picture you see, take a brush and, like an artist, dab on the colours which will delight your gaze.

Approach yourself as you would a clean canvas, and bring forth a masterpiece, skilfully producing a composition which will establish the beauty of your creation forever.

And if you wish, take a look at yourself through the eyes of a sculptor and see what can be extracted from this formless petrified boulder.

Create!

Go forward, My warrior, go forward and remember that infinite power is concealed within you and that divine might is embedded within your spirit.

Retreat not from obstacles, always remembering that you will stand on a higher rung by overcoming them.

Rise heavenwards, plunge into the mighty stream which bears the agglomeration of Fire, and you will find no one equal to you in might throughout the expanses of the Earth.

Go forward, My warrior, and remember that your steps are victorious and that each step affirms the Glory of the Empyreal World.

21 December

Many are called, a few have responded, and those who have reached Me are even fewer.

How is it that those following their chosen pathway suddenly turn off when they encounter the most insignificant obstacle on their path?

Is it not because they were looking at everything through rose-coloured spectacles?

Of course, you will not be treading upon petals of fragrant roses, but upon thorns and sharp spikes, for the Path of Love through the Earth has never been smooth for anyone.

PART II

This is why I tell you about bright wings that will help you transcend all obstacles and will allow you to preserve a feeling of Joy over the course of your laborious journey.

I am not calling you to a pleasure trip, but to heroic deeds for the sake of the triumph of Divine Love.

Respond, O man of the Earth and, if you feel that this cross is within your strength, share the burden of humanity, for you are ordained to follow the Pathway of Love.

Accept My Call, affirming its currents within your heart, knowing that it alone can help you reach Me.

We shall not constrain the weak by attempting to impose an excessive burden on them.

And only those who voluntarily offer their shoulders will receive a heavenly load — one they are able to bear.

And those who feel themselves even stronger may receive an even greater load to carry, in either the earthly world or the Empyreal.

The stellar burden is not for the weak-willed; it is intended for those strong in spirit, and only those will carry it who delight in the infinity of the path.

Trace the flight of your thought: did it fly as a dark arrow and pierce malicious offenders or, like a light-winged bird, did it touch their shoulder, bringing peace and calm where passions were raging.

Thought can awaken a dormant volcano; it can also pacify spews of hot lava.

Do not sprinkle ashes on either your own or someone else's head, but rather be concerned about keeping the sky above you clean; do not darken it by covering it with gloomy clouds.

Expand the horizon of your limited thinking by a fiery arrow and trace the most beautiful and divinely pure flight of your good thought; this will bring bliss into the world, glistening with the Light of Illumination.

Tell yourself what lies upon your heart, hidden under the bushel of your own unknown history.

Listen with sensitivity, asking the most intimate questions, and the Chalice of accumulations will stir forth, giving birth to clear answers.

It is necessary to know yourself — not with the aim of becoming conceited or self-deluded, nor to delve into mortal sins and despise yourself for past mistakes — but only so that, once you comprehend the truth, you can form the right impression and re-create yourself in the form you would like to see.

Tell yourself about the past, and you will be able to know what awaits you in the future.

PART II

Devastation threatens the world if Earth-dwellers do not tame the avarice of their appetites.

Why are you so callously cutting off the very branch on which you are sitting?

Come to your senses, good people, do not knock so vehemently with your axes, throw away your sharp instruments, pass your merciful hands over the wounds you have already inflicted, and water the deep cuts with your tears of bitter repentance — the world is yearning for healing; save it, and you yourselves will be cured of the terrifying madness that has taken such firm root in your minds.

You are ordained not to bring to ruin the world, but to increase its riches — always remember this.

The last Call has sounded, appealing to human reasonableness.

And a sigh of relief has passed through the whole planetary body, for it knows what is behind My Call.

The Armada of the approaching Fires will cleanse the Earth of rubbish, consuming all the debris of old structures in the raging Flame.

Neither dust nor rot will ever again prevent the body of the Earth from breathing.

And, once resurrected by the Power of Fire, the Earth will be able to regenerate all creation, showing forth a bright variety of divinely beautiful forms.

Truly wonderful is the moment of the New World's inception: the crucified Earth is preparing for her sacred resurrection and all Nature stands still in anticipation of a miracle of transfiguration, which your heart will witness.

Look vigilantly, listen keenly, and you will hear the magical melody of Love: this is Mother Earth responding to My Call with her whole heart; so you, too, must not hesitate to catch on to the tone of the marvellous resurrection, for it has sounded for the last time for you.

Geniuses are awakening and titans are emerging within simple human bodies.

The stellar step is reflected in the Earth, and its fiery grasp is visible to the darkness.

Heroes are advancing, holding firmly in their hands the victorious Banner of Light.

The path from man to God is being pursued on the Earth, and the miracle of transfiguration is ever more clearly seen to Us with every step you take.

Gods are being resurrected within your hearts, being born from the bowels of the awakened human genius.

PART II

22 December

Give away to the world everything you have.
And spare no light of your smile, but imbue every little petal with the breath of your loving heart.
You conceal countless riches within yourself; you carry them in your Chalice which is brimming over, yet it is hidden from sight.
But you yourself know what is stored in your recesses, and choosing the best, generously share the treasures of your stellar spirit, remembering that only those who have actually given away everything will be rewarded a thousandfold.

Close your eyes to others' shortcomings, but be sure to take note of all their achievements.
And even though you are aware of all your own achievements, close your eyes to them and take a closer look at your shortcomings.
Only in this way will you be able to eliminate selfishness, only thus will you firm up the gaze of your spiritual eye, which has remained closed for such a long time.

Approach yourself creatively.
The spirit is the creator; the body is your universe.
Look and see how fair the laws governing it are.

THE CALL OF THE HEART

And if they are not to your liking, institute other laws that will bring the Light of Transfiguration into all spheres of life.

Everything is within yourself!

Create!

The wealth of the world is multiplying, being combined by your wise hearts into a single treasury.

These are labouring day and night, without ever getting tired.

And the Light they are bringing is crystallizing every hour.

They who have enriched the treasury of the world have also unspeakably enriched themselves, but they will be capable of seeing their gifts only in the Ethereal Worlds, and these will surpass all expectations, for the human gaze cannot embrace all the wealth that will be prepared for their spirit.

Many dwellers of the Earth will depart as Ambassadors to Distant Worlds once they have been touched by the Light of the High Transfiguration.

They will need neither aircraft nor spacecraft nor special devices: a bright spirit will whirl them away into infinite stellar expanses, fulfilling the Mission of Love.

And no one will shut them out; on the contrary, all spheres will open wide with great joy, welcoming the Radiant Ambassadors — Ambassadors who do not know what evil is, for they will be imbued with the currents of Divine Love alone.

Rely upon yourself or, rather, upon your heart: it will show you the only right path leading towards the Light.

And do not go accepting the rationality of brain-provided arguments; do not choose your path according to someone else's suggestions, for they can throw you off track and lead you far astray from your unified goal.

You have a counsellor, a companion, and a wise saviour — it is your flaming heart.

It knows everything and is aware of all the mysteries of the earthly world as well as of the Empyreal.

Know that it is only your human heart — containing within itself the fiery seed — that We can rely upon, and so you, too, can rely upon that which is inviolable for ever.

The Call of the Age of Aquarius has sounded within your heart.

Have you heard it?

Have you beheld the entire Beauty of the New World which is beginning to emerge on your lands?

Have you admitted to your soul My Word, which is full of great simplicity?

Answer these questions to yourself and if the spirit of affirmation touches you — form the rungs of ascent together with Me.

The first rung is brought to your earthly feet; plant yourself firmly upon it, and direct your gaze to the next one, for the Light of Illumination is hastening to fill your heart.

If you have heard the Call of the Heart, then follow your heart!

I have spoken.

Maitreya

*They will ask you: "How does one master a new rung?"
Answer: "Only through a heart full of the unified
fiery aspiration to reach the shore of Light
will you take a step towards Love."*

BOOK 2
The Illumination of the Heart

SPIRITUAL ILLUMINATION awaits everyone who has responded to the Call of the Heart. Now it is time to unveil before your eyes an unprecedented Mystery, which until this time has remained the Secret of Secrets.

"The entrance of the Messiah in this period — 1998," predicted the prominent prophet Edgar Cayce in 1932. His prediction accurately came true, but very few people knew about this... *until now*.

Where and how did the Messiah descend into the earthly world, predicted long ago, but wholly unnoticed?

In Book 2 of *The Teaching of the Heart*, the Lord, for the first time in history, unveils this Secret. He entrusts all human hearts to witness the greatest and most unprecedented Miracle of the Divine Incarnation of His Son, which took place in 1998 within several worlds as the first stage of the Advent.

However, not only will you behold this Miracle as if through your own eyes, but you will also experience it within your own heart. As you read the powerfully poetic pages of this book, an imperceptible mystery will occur inside you: the Divine Love of the Lord will transfigure the essence of your entire being, preparing you to become a particle of His human entity at the time of the Great Advent.

Offering spiritual food for further deep reflections, Book 2 of *The Teaching of the Heart* continues to provide you with inspirational and illuminating instructions from the Lord of Love and Compassion to transform the whole world through self-perfection.

Learn more at: www.dushkova.com/en

THANK YOU FOR READING!

If you enjoyed this book, please consider leaving a review, even if it is only a line or two. It would make all the difference and would be very much appreciated.

Sign up for our newsletter to be the first to know when new books by Zinovia Dushkova are published:

www.dushkova.com/en/sign-up

NOTES

1. One of the Tibetan prophecies about Shambhala and Maitreya says:

"One two three! I see three books of the coming of Maitreya. The first is written in the West. The second is written in the East. The third will be written in the North."

Nicholas Roerich, *Heart of Asia* (Rochester, VT: Inner Traditions, 1990), p. 97.

"The Ruler of Shambhala reveals three Doctrines to humanity."

Helena Roerich, *Hierarchy* (New York: Agni Yoga Society, 1977), pp. 13–14.

2. See *Lost Book of Nostradamus*, directed by Kreg Lauterbach (Los Angeles: History Channel, 2008), DVD.

3. Thomas Edison was a member of the Theosophical Society, which was founded by Helena Blavatsky in 1875.

4. According to Marc Seifer's well-researched biography of Nikola Tesla, Tesla also studied Blavatsky's works, from which he drew the idea of the *Akashic Records*, or the spatial Treasury of Knowledge; the substance of Akasha is an eternal source of energy, which he used for his inventions. See Marc Seifer, *Wizard* (New York: Citadel Press, 2001), p. 164.

5. According to Eunice Layton and Jack Brown, Albert Einstein always had a copy of Blavatsky's *The Secret Doctrine* on his desk. See Sylvia Cranston, *H.P.B.* (New York: Jeremy P. Tarcher, 1994), pp. 557–558; Jack Brown, "I Visit Professor Einstein," *Ojai Valley News* (28 September 1983).

6. The 9th Panchen Lama endorsed Blavatsky's *The Voice of the Silence*, published in 1927 by the Chinese Buddhist Research Society in Peking.

7. The 14th Dalai Lama wrote a foreword to the centenary edition of *The Voice of the Silence*, published in 1989 by Concord Grove Press, Santa Barbara.

Furthermore, according to the reminiscence of Vsevolod Ovchinnikov, a Russian journalist, on 14

September 1955, when he had a private audience with the Dalai Lama, he said to Ovchinnikov: "I am glad to have finally met a compatriot of Madame Blavatsky — her works are highly appreciated by our scholars."

Vsevolod Ovchinnikov, "Sootechestvennik Blavatskoi" [A compatriot of Blavatsky], *Rossiyskaya Gazeta*, no. 3154 (1 March 2003).

8. "At the close of each 'great year,' called by Aristotle — according to Censorinus — the *greatest*, and which consists of six *sars* our planet is subjected to a thorough physical revolution. The polar and equatorial climates gradually exchange places; the former moving slowly toward the Line, and the tropical zone, with its exuberant vegetation and swarming animal life, replacing the forbidding wastes of the icy poles. This change of climate is necessarily attended by cataclysms, earthquakes, and other cosmical throes."

Helena Blavatsky, *Isis Unveiled*, vol. 1 (New York: J. W. Bouton, 1877), pp. 30–31.

"Our globe is subject to seven periodical entire changes which go *pari passu* with the races. For the Secret Doctrine teaches that, during this Round, there must be seven terrestrial *pralayas*, three occasioned by the change in the inclination of the earth's axis. It is a *law* which acts at its appointed time, and not at all blindly, as science may think, but in strict accordance and harmony with *Karmic* law. In Occultism this inexorable law is referred to as 'the great Adjuster.' Science confesses its ignorance of the cause producing climatic vicissitudes and such changes in the axial direction, which are always followed by these vicissitudes; nor does it seem so sure of the axial changes. And being unable to account for them, it is prepared rather to deny the axial phenomena altogether, than admit the intelligent Karmic hand and law which alone could reasonably explain such sudden changes and their results."

Helena Blavatsky, *The Secret Doctrine*, vol. 2 (London: Theosophical Publishing Company, 1888), pp. 329–330.

"Climates will, and have already begun to, change, each tropical year after the other dropping one sub-race, but only to beget another higher race on the ascending cycle."

Helena Blavatsky, *The Secret Doctrine*, vol. 2 (London: Theosophical Publishing Company, 1888), p. 446.

9. "Maitreya is the secret name of the *Fifth* Buddha, and the *Kalki* Avatar of the Brahmins — the last Messiah who will come at the culmination of the Great Cycle."

Helena Blavatsky, *The Secret Doctrine*, vol. 1 (London: Theosophical Publishing Company, 1888), p. 384.

"Millenarians and Adventists of robust faith, may go on saying that 'the coming of (the carnalised) Christ' is near at hand, and prepare themselves for 'the end of the world.' Theosophists — at any rate, some of them — who understand the hidden meaning of the universally-expected Avatars, Messiahs, Sosioshes and Christs — know that it is no 'end of the world,' but 'the consummation of the age,' i.e., the close of a cycle, which is now fast approaching."

Helena Blavatsky, *Collected Writings*, vol. 8 (Wheaton, IL: Theosophical Publishing House, 1956), pp. 173–174.

"The simple secret is this: There are cycles within greater cycles, which are all contained in the one Kalpa of 4,320,000 years. It is at the end of this cycle that the Kalki-Avatâra is expected — the Avatâra whose name and characteristics are secret, who will come forth from Shambhala, the 'City of Gods,' which is in the West for some nations, in the East for others, in the North or South for yet others. And this is the reason why, from the Indian Rishi to Virgil, and from Zoroaster down to the latest Sibyl, all have, since the beginning of the Fifth Race, prophesied, sung, and promised the cyclic return of the Virgin — Virgo, the constellation — and the birth of a divine child who should bring back to our earth the Golden Age."

Helena Blavatsky, *Collected Writings*, vol. 14 (Wheaton, IL: Theosophical Publishing House, 1982), p. 354.

10. Mahatma Koot Hoomi, one of the Great Teachers, wrote in the autumn 1881:

"Notwithstanding that the time is not quite ripe to let you entirely into the secret; and that you are hardly yet prepared to understand the great Mystery, even if told of it, owing to the great injustice and wrong done, I am empowered to allow you a glimpse behind the veil. This state of [Helena Blavatsly] is intimately connected with her occult training in Tibet, and due to her being sent out alone into the world to gradually prepare the way for others. After nearly a century of fruitless search, our chiefs had to avail themselves of the only opportunity to send out a European *body* upon European soil to serve as a connecting link between that country and our own. You do not understand? Of course not. Please then, remember, what she tried to explain, and what you gathered tolerably well from her, namely the fact of the *seven* principles in the *complete* human being. Now, no man or woman, unless he be an initiate of the 'fifth circle,' can leave the precincts of *Bod-Las* and return back into the world in his integral whole — if I may use the expression. One, at least of his seven satellites has to remain behind for two reasons: the first to form the necessary connecting link, the wire of transmission — the second as the safest warranter that certain things will never be divulged."

The Mahatma Letters to A. P. Sinnett, comp. Trevor Baker (Pasadena, CA: Theosophical University Press, 1992), p. 203.

11. "In century the twentieth, some disciple more informed, and far better fitted, may be sent by the Masters of Wisdom."

Helena Blavatsky, *The Secret Doctrine*, vol. 1 (London: Theosophical Publishing Company, 1888), p. xxxviii.

12. "Let us not forget that many interpretations were wrong, for their meaning was deliberately obscured and the Forces of Light did not even seek to clarify them until a certain time, because they saw the treachery that was in the works. The period of 1936 was great, for it marked the end of a particular regime. It was a great victory for the Forces of Light. It is also interesting to note that now the year 1942 as the end of Kali Yuga and the incarnation of the Kalki Avatar in Shambhala is broadly being accepted across India. This period is correct. Our Teacher indicated it long ago. Pundits are now proving that the large numbers in the Scriptures were concealment and they should be counted not as years, but as days, and then the period of the end of

Kali Yuga falls in 1942. This is quite correct, for you can find a statement in *The Secret Doctrine* that zeros are often used to hide real numbers. Also, the end of Kali Yuga esoterically should coincide with the entry into the Cycle of Aquarius." (3 December 1937)

Helena Roerich, *Pis'ma* [Letters], vol. 5 (Moscow: Mezhdunarodnyi tsentr Rerikhov, 2003), p. 324.

"Today a solar eclipse is taking place. Kali Yuga ended on 1 August and Satya Yuga is coming into force. Such are the calculations of the Brahmins. They even published a small book, which, for some reason, is prohibited by the [Indian] government." (1 August 1943)

Nicholas Roerich, *Listy dnevnika* [Diary leaves], vol. 3 (Moscow: Mezhdunarodnyi tsentr Rerikhov, 2002), p. 130.

"A letter from a lama in Kalimpong. On 1 August, in all Buddhist temples solemn services were held to mark the end of the dark age of Kali Yuga and the beginning of the light age, Satya Yuga. On 15 August, Rigden Dragpo, the Avatar of Light, goes to fight for the truth, for the building of a new world. A long-awaited event! These periods have also been celebrated and recorded in Tibet and Mongolia. Shambhala is on everyone's lips. How greatly people waited for 1943! But they understood that events occur gradually. There can be no instant transformations. Only avalanches and earthquakes thunder suddenly, unexpected." (17 August 1943)

Nicholas Roerich, *Listy dnevnika* [Diary leaves], vol. 3 (Moscow: Mezhdunarodnyi tsentr Rerikhov, 2002), p. 135.

13. Some of Helena Roerich's letters to President Roosevelt are now stored in the Franklin D. Roosevelt Presidential Library and Museum in Hyde Park, NY.

14. "In the new era, there will be many that are called mediators; of course, such assistants will be able to help to shift consciousness away from the dead point of negations." (28 April 1951)

Helena Roerich, *Pis'ma* [Letters], vol. 9 (Moscow: Mezhdunarodnyi tsentr Rerikhov, 2009), pp. 37–38.

15. "It is also necessary to pass on the foundations of the Fiery Experience. Many people at the end of our century will come to it, and one of the Sisters of the Brotherhood will be my successor, and she will carry out Agni Yoga under new and, possibly, improved conditions." (10 October 1954)

Helena Roerich, *Pis'ma* [Letters], vol. 9 (Moscow: Mezhdunarodnyi tsentr Rerikhov, 2009), p. 468.

NOTES

16. Helena Roerich's *Brotherhood* was published in English by Agni Yoga Society, New York, as five books: *Brotherhood* and four parts of *Supermundane*.

17. Mitar Tarabich (1829–1899), a prominent Serbian prophet, foresaw for the second half of the 20th century and present time:

"Among people of a nation far in the North, a little man will appear who will teach men about Love and Compassion, but there will be many hypocrites around him so that he will have many ups and downs. Not one of these hypocrites will want to know what is real human grace, but his wise books will remain and all the words he will say, and then people will see how self-deceived they were."

Neo, ed., "The Prophecies of Mitar Tarabich," *Nexus Magazine*, vol. 13, no. 1 (December 2005–January 2006), p. 78.

18. "For changes are coming, this may be sure — an evolution, or revolution in the ideas of religious thought. The basis of it for the world will eventually come out of Russia; not communism, no! But rather that which is the basis of the same, as the Christ taught — His kind of communism!" (29 November 1932)

"Out of Russia, you see, there may come that which may be the basis of a more worldwide religious thought or trend." (25 August 1933)

"In Russia there comes the hope of the world, not as that sometimes termed of the Communistic, of the Bolshevistic; no. But freedom, freedom! That each man will live for his fellow man!" (22 June 1944)

Edgar Cayce, *The Complete Edgar Cayce Readings* (Virginia Beach, VA: A.R.E. Press, 2006), CD-ROM, Readings 452–6, 3976–12, 3976–29.

19. In 1978, Vanga (1911–1996), a famous Bulgarian prophetess, predicted that the New Teaching of the White Brotherhood would appear in Russia in 1998:

"The New Teaching will come from Russia. That country will be the first to be purged. The White Brotherhood will spread across Russia and from there its Teaching will begin its march throughout the world. This will happen in twenty years — it will not happen earlier. In twenty years, you will reap the first rich harvest."

Zheni Kostadinova, *Vanga* (Moscow: AST, 1998), pp. 71–72.

20. Horace Hayman Wilson, trans., *The Vishnu Purana* (London: 1840), p. 484.

21. Sung Mo Koo, trans., "The Korean Books of Prophecy," *Who is He?*, http://www.tparents.org/moon-books/cta-ik/Cta-ik-6-2.htm.

22. Helena Blavatsky, *The Theosophical Glossary* (London: Theosophical Publishing Society, 1892), p. 287.

23. See Zinovia Dushkova, *The Book of Secret Wisdom* (Moscow: Radiant Books, 2015), p. 103.

24. Huilin's *Sounds and Meanings of all the Buddhist Scriptures* says:

"The udumbara flower is the product of propitious and supernatural phenomena; it is a celestial flower and does not exist in the mundane world. If a Tathagata or the King of the Golden Wheel appears in the human world, this flower will appear due to his great virtue and blessings."

Tara MacIsaac, "Flower Said to Bloom Once in 3,000 Years Spotted Across Globe," *Epoch Times*, http://www.theepochtimes.com/n3/725095-flower-said-to-bloom-once-in-3000-years-spotted-across-globe/.

25. "The entrance of the Messiah in this period — 1998." (30 June 1932)

Edgar Cayce, *The Complete Edgar Cayce Readings* (Virginia Beach, VA: A.R.E. Press, 2006), CD-ROM, Reading 5748–5.

26. See Zinovia Dushkova, *The Book of Secret Wisdom* (Moscow: Radiant Books, 2015), pp. 100–110.

NOTES

27. See, for example, William Frederick, "The Sign of the Woman Clothed with the Sun in 2017," *The End Times Forecaster*, http://endtimesforecaster.blogspot.com/2013/06/2017-and-woman-clothed-with-sun.html.

28. Edward Conze, trans., *Buddhist Scriptures* (Harmondsworth, Middlesex: Penguin Books, 1959), p. 239.

29. Rev. 12:1–2.

30. See Daniel Matson, "The Oracle in Stone," *Signs of the End*, http://watchfortheday.org/signsoftheend/giza2024.html.

31. "Some 800 years ago in Germany, Rabbi Judah Ben Samuel was a top Talmudic scholar with an inclination for the mystical. Before he died in the year 1217, he prophesied that the Ottoman Turks would conquer Jerusalem and rule the Holy City for 'eight jubilee years.' A biblical jubilee year consists of 50 years. Fifty multiplied by eight equals 400 years. Afterwards, according to Ben Samuel, the Ottomans would be driven out of Jerusalem, which would remain no-man's land for one jubilee year. In the tenth jubilee year, Jerusalem would return to the Jewish people and then the Messianic end times would begin."

Ludwig Schneider, "Israel: Between Mysticism and Reality," *Israel Today*, no. 110 (March 2008), p. 18.

32. "Vtoroe prishestvie Khrista sostoitsia 22-go oktiabria 2017-go goda" [The Second Coming of Christ will take place on 22 October 2017], http://221017.ru/sample-page.

33. "Count two or three decades after the decades of Hijri 1400. At that time, the Mahdi emerges."

Harun Yahya, *The Signs of Prophet Jesus' (pbuh) Second Coming* (Istanbul: Global Publishing, 2004), p. 414.

34. "And there is none of the People of the Book but must believe in him before his death; and on the Day of Judgement he will be a witness against them." (Quran 4:159)

35. Harun Yahya, *The Signs of Prophet Jesus' (pbuh) Second Coming* (Istanbul: Global Publishing, 2004), pp. 433–434.

36. Cavan Sieczkowski, "St. Malachy Last Pope Prophecy: What Theologians Think About 12th-Century Prediction," *The Huffington Post*, 14 February 2013, http://www.huffingtonpost.com/2013/02/14/st-malachy-last-pope-prophecy-theologians-prediction-_n_2679662.html.

37. Matt. 24:22.

38. "The Hour will not begin until time passes quickly, so a year will be like a month, and a month will be like a week, and a week will be like a day, and a day will be like an hour, and an hour will be like the burning of a braid of palm leaves."

Islam Question and Answer, http://islamqa.info/en/34618.

39. See, for example, this news report: "Rare Buddhist flower found under nun's washing machine," *The Telegraph*, 1 March 2010, http://www.telegraph.co.uk/news/worldnews/asia/china/7345137/Rare-Buddhist-flower-found-under-nuns-washing-machine.html.

40. "The 17 warmest years on record have all occurred in the last 18 years."

LuAnn Dahlman, "Climate Change: Global Temperature," *Climate.gov*, http://www.climate.gov/news-features/understanding-climate/climate-change-global-temperature.

See also "GISS Surface Temperature Analysis," *NASA*, http://data.giss.nasa.gov/gistemp/graphs_v3.

41. According to EM-DAT, the total number of natural disasters reported each year has been steadily increasing in recent decades, from 30 in 1955 to 375 in 2015.

See "Disaster Trends," *EM-DAT*, http://www.emdat.be/disaster_trends/index.html.

42. An Associated Press survey in 1997 revealed that 24% of American adults expected to be still alive when Jesus returns. A poll conducted for Newsweek magazine in June 1999 showed that 52% of American adults believed that Jesus would return during the next millennium — i.e., between years 2001 and 3000. A 2010 Pew Research poll reported that 41% of Americans believe that Jesus Christ will have returned to the Earth by the year 2050.

B. A. Robinson, "Americans' Beliefs about God's Existence and Importance; Jesus' Second Coming," *Ontario Consultants on Religious Tolerance*, http://www.religioustolerance.org/godpoll.htm.

Pew Research Center, "Jesus Christ's Return to Earth," 14 July 2010, http://www.pewresearch.org/daily-number/jesus-christs-return-to-earth.

GLOSSARY

If you would like to understand more deeply the simple words and phrases used in the books of *The Teaching of the Heart*, please refer to the comprehensive esoteric glossary included in *The Book of Secret Wisdom*.

Chalice — the fourth energy centre, or *chakra*, also known as *Anahata*; located in the heart on the subtle plane. It is in the Chalice that memories about all the past lives are stored and that the energy crystal known as *Ringse* is formed.

Esoteric (*Greek*, "inner") — hidden, secret.

God — the Divine, Unchangeable, Invariable, and Infinite Principle; the eternally Unknowable Cause of All that exists; omnipresent, all-pervading, visible and invisible spiritual Nature, which exists everywhere, in which everything lives, moves, and has its being; the Absolute, including the potential of all things as well as all universal manifestations. Upon being made manifest, out of its Absolute Oneness God becomes the Absolute of infinite differentiation and its consequences — relativity and opposites. God has no gender and cannot be imagined as a human being. In the Holy Scriptures, God is Fire, God is Love — the one primeval energy that conceives the worlds.

The traditional Christian concept of *God* refers to a *Demiurge* (*Greek*, "creator") — God the Creator or the Lord of a certain world in the Universe. This is a High Spirit, who has passed His human evolution and who is now responsible together with other Spirits for the evolution and construction of this particular world. Each planet, star system, and galaxy, just as the whole Universe, has their Demiurges that form the unified Hierarchy of Light. Seven Great Lords headed by the Lord M. are the Demiurges of the planet Earth, and these are subordinate to the Demiurge of the Solar System — the Solar Hierarch.

Gods — the Spirits of the Higher Spheres, Distant Worlds, who have succeeded in achieving a high level of evolution, far surpassing the level of earthly people that led to human beings beginning to

GLOSSARY

perceive them as Gods. In other words, this level of spiritual achievement is destined for man as well. The Seven High Spirits are responsible for the development of humanity on the planet Earth; they assumed a human appearance to raise people's consciousness.

Kali Yuga (*Sanskrit*, "Dark Age") — an era of spiritual decline and ignorance. Esoterically, Kali Yuga ended in 1942, the year when the Lord Maitreya was incarnated in Shambhala.

Karma (*Sanskrit*, "action") — the Cosmic Law of Cause and Effect, which is expressed in the formula, "as you sow, so shall you reap"; defines the frames within which the destiny of an individual, people, planet, and so on can be developed.

Maitreya Sangha* (*Sanskrit*, "Community of Maitreya") — the Sign of Maitreya; the Sign of the Era of Love; the Sign of the Heart. Also means the network of the invisible Abodes of the Great Teachers, which are spread out high in the Himalayas, encircling the Chief Stronghold, where the Temple of the Lord of Shambhala is located.

Maya (*Sanskrit*, "illusion") — the illusive and transient nature of earthly reality and existence.

---

* Appears as the symbol on the cover of this book.

GLOSSARY

Mahatma (*Sanskrit*, "Great Soul") — the title often used to refer to the Great Teachers of humanity, who, after achieving full control over their nature, possess extraordinary wisdom and spiritual powers.

Planetary Spirit — the Supreme Lord or Ruler of a planet. As a rule, the governing Hierarchy of Light for young planets, such as the Earth, consists of High Spirits that came from Distant Worlds, wherein they long ago had gone through the given planet's stage of Evolution. When the humankind of such a planet reaches spiritual maturity, the Lords of Light who arrived from other Worlds leave it, to be replaced by worthy High Spirits who have already gone through their evolution on that young planet.

From ancient sacred texts, it is evident that the Planetary Spirit of the Earth is the Lord of Sirius. Besides, even the Quran states that Allah is the Lord of Sirius. However, it should be borne in mind that the God described in the Old Testament is not the Supreme Lord of the Earth whom Christ calls His Father in the New Testament.

Unfolding in present times, the Nativity Mystery of the Planetary Spirit of Sirius in the Glorious Body on the Higher Planes of the Earth will occur

GLOSSARY

for the first time on the planet. It is of great significance not only for the Earth and the Solar System, but also for all the constellations headed by Sirius. This Mystery of Light will never be repeated in the present Grand Cycle of Evolution.

Ringse (*Tibetan*, "treasure") — a crystal in the human body that is formed through the deposition of energies when an individual lives a highly moral life and serves people. It becomes visible after cremation. Such crystals are displayed at the *Maitreya Loving Kindness* exhibition.

Satya Yuga (*Sanskrit*, "Light Age") — the Golden Age, the era of truth and awakening of spirituality; corresponds to the Age of Aquarius. Esoterically, Satya Yuga began in 1942, the year when the Lord Maitreya was incarnated in Shambhala.

Senzar (*Senzar*, "language of the Sun") — the sacred language spoken by the members of Shambhala, in which the oldest manuscripts, such as the secret *Book of Dzyan*, are written. It is taught in secret schools of the East.

Shambhala (*Sanskrit*, "Place of Peace") — the Chief Abode of Light in the heart of the Himalayas. Different peoples identify various places for it, and there is also a truth to this, because the network of the Abodes of Shambhala is spread not only throughout the Himalayas, but also within other mountainous and remote locations around the world.

Tactica Adversa (*Latin*, "adverse") — a tactic from the reverse, which ensures success for the Forces of Light in the worst conditions, i.e., it allows them to benefit from the worst circumstances.

Tushita (*Sanskrit*, "Heavens of Joy") — the Supreme Fiery Spheres, where High Spirits abide and from where they descend in order to be incarnated on the Earth; the Shambhala of the Supreme Spheres.

More information can be found in the esoteric glossary of *The Book of Secret Wisdom*.

ABOUT THE AUTHOR

Zinovia Dushkova, Ph.D., is a Russian author, poet, philosopher, historian, and traveller. She has been honoured with a number of awards, prizes, and commendations for her contribution to the spiritual development of society and for merit in the domain of scientific research in the ecology of consciousness. She is a Fellow of the European Academy of Natural Sciences and the European Scientific Society, both based in Hanover, Germany.

Dr. Dushkova's interest in the history of world religions and philosophy, along with a desire to realize and fulfil her mission in life, led her first to the wisdom of prominent philosophers and thinkers, and

ABOUT THE AUTHOR

subsequently to the works of Helena Blavatsky and the Roerichs, which changed her life radically. It is said in Oriental teachings that when the disciple is ready, the Teacher will appear — thus, in 1992, the Master came to her. After three years of intense training and probation, in 1995 she embarked on her first trip to India — the land of ancient teachings. There, at the foot of the sacred Himalayas, in the Buddhist Ghoom Monastery — where Madame Blavatsky in 1882 and Helena Roerich in 1923 met with the Master M. — the path of Zinovia Dushkova began.

The mysterious paths — leading into the heart of the Himalayas and the Blue Mountains, in the vicinity of Mounts Kanchenjunga, Kailash, Everest, and so on — brought Dushkova to the secret Abodes of Light, from where the Call had sounded. Much like a hermit monk, she started poring over the sacred manuscripts that had been preserved in the most hidden corners of Sikkim, Ladakh, and other unexplored places of India. Thus, she gained admittance to the secret *Book of Dzyan*, the stanzas of which were first revealed by Helena Blavatsky, forming the basis of *The Secret Doctrine*. A new excerpt from this mysterious manuscript was later published in *The Book of Secret Wisdom*.

Dr. Dushkova has devoted almost 25 years of her life to the study and acquisition of hidden esoteric wisdom, which she is now sharing with people through her books. She is the author of approximately forty works, published in Russia, Ukraine, Moldova, and France. These works of an ethical and spiritual nature reflect a synthesis of science, religion, history, and philosophy. Underlying her poetry and prose, fairy tales and legends, is a worldview full of wisdom and the cultural heritage of both the East and the West.

Zinovia Dushkova's major works, *The Teaching of the Heart*, *The Fiery Bible*, and *The Secret Doctrine of Love*, have called forth a wave of social movement in Russia, Ukraine, and Kazakhstan, centred around the development of culture, science, and education, all of which contribute to the progress and prosperity of society. Her award-winning philosophical children's book, *Fairy Tales for the Saviour*, has been given a ringing endorsement by teachers working with problem children in orphanages and juvenile detention centres.

**Visit the author's official website
and sign up for a newsletter at:**
www.dushkova.com/en

Follow the author at:
www.facebook.com/ZinoviaDushkova
www.twitter.com/ZinoviaDushkova
www.goodreads.com/ZinoviaDushkova

ALSO BY THE AUTHOR

THE BOOK OF SECRET WISDOM

Hidden away for long millennia, the world's most ancient sacred text reveals the past, present, and future of humanity.

A million years ago, the Great Masters of Wisdom recorded a mysterious manuscript widely known as the *Book of Dzyan* — a Tibetan name meaning the *Book of Secret Wisdom*. Written in a language unfamiliar to modern philology, called *Senzar*, this oldest book in the world has served as the source of every ancient religion, philosophy, and science.

The Masters stored it in the legendary realm of Shambhala, each century admitting only a few chosen ones to read some of its pages. Now a new excerpt from the *Book of Dzyan*, consisting of twelve stanzas and supplemented with exclusive material, is published in English for the first time. Reading through the pages of this work, you will be able to trace the whole course of the spiritual evolution of humanity and our Earth beyond Time and Space.

Learn more at: www.dushkova.com/en

ALSO BY THE AUTHOR

PARABLES FROM SHAMBHALA

This inspirational collection of twelve profound parables reveals the greatest ancient truths of the East, which will be helpful to everyone on their path of self-improvement and spiritual growth.

During her trips across Tibet, India, Nepal, and Mongolia, Zinovia Dushkova has stayed at numerous monasteries — those open to the public as well as those hidden high within mountains and caves. Representatives of different religions, elderly monks and hermits, generously shared secret knowledge with her. In the course of their conversations, they narrated legends and tales originating from the mysterious kingdom of Shambhala. These experiences served as an inspiration to the author. Thus, in 2004, under the canopy of gigantic deodar cedars on one of the summits of the Himalayas, she started writing down this book of parables.

Learn more at: www.dushkova.com/en

Made in the USA
San Bernardino, CA
17 December 2018